Published by:
Airlife Publishing Ltd
101 Longden Road
Shrewsbury SY3 9EB
England
Telephone: 01743 235651
Fax: 01743 232944

Produced by Aerospace Publishing Ltd and
published jointly with Airlife Publishing Ltd

© Aerospace Publishing Ltd 1995

Design:
Karen Leverington

Editorial Assistant:
Tim Senior

First published 1995

ISBN 1 85310 586 4

Printed in Singapore

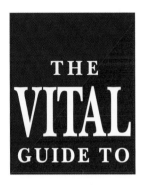

THE VITAL GUIDE TO

FIGHTING AIRCRAFT OF WORLD WAR II

EDITOR: KAREN LEVERINGTON

Airlife
England

Aichi D3A 'Val'

Famous for its part in the attack on Pearl Harbor, and later for its sinking of the British carrier HMS Hermes and cruisers HMS Cornwall and Devonshire, the Aichi D3A mirrored the Japanese approach to the 'Stuka' concept. This D3A1 Model 11 served with the Yokosuka Kokutai in 1940.

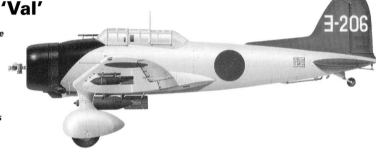

Although thought to be obsolescent when Japan entered the war, the **Aichi D3A** with fixed spatted landing gear was the first Japanese aircraft to drop bombs on American targets when aircraft of this type took part in the great raid on Pearl Harbor on 7 December 1941. Designed to a 1936 carrier-based dive-bomber requirement, the prototype was flown in January 1938 with a 710-hp (430-kW) Nakajima Hikari 1 radial. Production **D3A1**s had slightly smaller wings and were powered by the 1,000-hp (746-kW) Mitsubishi Kinsei 43 radial. A dorsal fin extension considerably improved the aircraft's manoeuvrability, although the armament of only two forward-firing 7.7-mm (0.303-in) machine-guns, with another of the same calibre in the rear cockpit, was insufficient. After limited land-based operations in China and Indo-China, D3A1s were flown in all major carrier actions during the first 10 months of the war and sank more Allied naval vessels than any other Axis aircraft. Among British casualties in D3A1 attacks were HMS *Hermes* (the world's first carrier to be sunk by carrier aircraft), and the cruisers HMS *Cornwall* and HMS *Dorsetshire*. Heavy losses among D3A1s during and after the Battle of the Coral Sea, however, forced withdrawal by most of the survivors to land bases. In 1942 the **D3A2** was introduced, featuring increased fuel capacity and more powerful engine, but by 1944 the aircraft were hopelessly outclassed by American fighters; a small number were subsequently employed in *kamikaze* attacks. Production amounted to 476 D3A1s and 1,016 D3A2s. The Allied reporting name was 'Val'.

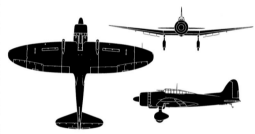

Aichi D3A 'Val'

Despite their many successes in the early months of the Pacific war, many of the Japanese aircraft, such as the Aichi D3A dive-bomber, were obsolescent by European standards but were marginally superior to anything the British and Americans had available in the Far East, and were present in far greater numbers.

Specification:
Aichi D3A2
Type: two-seat shipborne dive-bomber
Powerplant: one 1,300-hp (970-kW) Mitsubishi Kinsei 54 radial piston
Performance: max speed 267 mph (430 km/h) at 20,340 ft (6200 m); climb to 9,845 ft (3000 m) in 5.76 minutes; service ceiling 34,450 ft (10500 m); range 840 miles (1352 km)
Weights: empty 5,666 lb (2570 kg); max take-off 8,378 lb (3800 kg)
Dimensions: span 47 ft 2 in (14.38 m); length 33 ft 5⅜ in (10.20 m); height 12 ft 7½ in (3.85 m); wing area 375.7 sq ft (34.9 m²)
Armament: two 7.7-mm (0.303-in) Type 97 machine-guns in nose, one 7.7-mm (0.303-in) Type 92 gun in rear cockpit; one 551-lb (250-kg) bomb under fuselage

Arado Ar 234

An Arado Ar 234B-2 of 9.KG 76 commanded by Major Hans-Georg Batcher and based at Pheine and Achmer. II/KG 76 became fully operational in February 1945, losing its first aircraft in action on 24 February with P-47s near Segelsdorf.

Delayed by slow delivery of the Junkers 004B turbojets, the **Arado Ar 234 V1** prototype was not first flown until 15 June 1943; this aircraft featured an auxiliary trolley, which was jettisoned on take-off, in place of conventional landing gear. Additional prototypes followed, including the Ar 234**V6** and **V8** which were powered by four 1,764 lb (7.85-kN) thrust BMW 003A-1 turbojets. When production finally started, it was of the twin-jet **Ar 234B** which featured conventional nosewheel landing gear, the mainwheels retracting into a slightly widened centre fuselage. The **Ar 234B-1** was an unarmed reconnaissance aircraft which first served with 1 /Versuchsverband Oberbefehlshaber der Luftwaffe late in 1944, and soon after with Sonderkommando Hecht and Sperling. These units were replaced in 1945 by 1 (F)/33, 1 (F)/100 and 1 (F)/123, and many reconnaissance sorties were flown over the UK. The bomber version was the **Ar 234B-2**, which could carry a bomb load of 4,409 lb (200 kg), and other variants included the **Ar 234B-2/b** reconnaissance aircraft, the **Ar 234B-2/1** pathfinder and **Ar 234B-2/r** long-range bomber. Ar 234B-2 bombers joined KG 76 in January 1945 and carried out a number of hazardous raids before the end of the war. A small number of Ar 234s were also employed as night-fighters with Kommando Bonow, but the four-jet **Ar 234C**, although beginning to appear at the end of the war, failed to reach squadron service. Other projects were in hand when hostilities ceased.

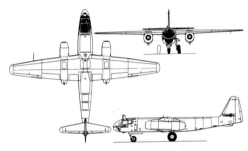

Arado Ar 234B-2

Specification: Arado Ar 234B-2
Type: single-seat tactical light bomber
Powerplant: two 1,764-lb (7.85-kN) thrust BMW 003A-1 turbojets
Performance: max speed 461 mph (742 km/h) at 19,685 ft (6000 m); climb to 19,685 ft (6000 m) in 12.8 minutes; service ceiling 32,810 ft (10000 m); range 1,013 miles (1630 km)
Weights: empty 11,464 lb (5200 kg); max take-off 21,605 lb (9800 kg)
Dimensions: span 46 ft 3½ in (14.44 m); length 41 ft 5½ in (12.64 m); height 14 ft 1½ in (4.29 m); wing area 284.17 sq ft (27.3 m²)
Armament: bomb load of up to 4,409 lb (2000 kg); some aircraft carried two rear-firing 20-mm guns

The world's first turbojet-powered bomber, the Arado Ar 234 Blitz (Lightning) was originally conceived late in 1940 as a twin-jet high-speed reconnaissance aircraft. Their high speed rendered them immune to interception.

Armstrong Whitworth Albemarle

An Armstrong Whitworth Albemarle Mk V special transport of No. 297 Sqn, RAF, normally based at Stoney Cross, but flown out to the Mediterranean to participate in the airborne assault on Sicily that month.

Performing the lesser known but vital tasks of glider tug and paratrooping pathfinder and troop transport, the **Armstrong Whitworth Albemarle** was originally designed to a 1938 medium bomber requirement, using a composite construction of wood and steel, intended to facilitate sub-contract manufacture outside the aircraft industry. The first prototype crashed, and the second flew on 20 March 1940, being followed by 32 aircraft produced as bombers but not accepted as such by the RAF. Repeated changes in A. W. Hawkesley's production line caused by numerous modifications delayed delivery to the RAF until January 1943, by which time the Hercules XI-powered Albemarle **Mk I** was being produced as a special transport for use by the airborne forces. Albemarle Mk II glider tugs, plus Albemarle **Mks II**, **V** and **VI** special transports followed, together with Albemarle Mk VI glider tugs. Only one Wright Double Cyclone-powered Albemarle **Mk IV** was built. Production of the Albemarle totalled 602, of which a small number were supplied to Russia. The glider tug first went into action towing Horsa gliders during the invasion of Sicily, and during the Normandy landings of 6 June 1944 flew as pathfinders for the 6th Airborne Division, dropping men of the 22nd Independent Parachute Company; later, they towed gliders during the Arnhem operation. In all, Albemarles equipped seven RAF squadrons.

Armstrong Whitworth Albemarle

Despite production delays, the Albemarle came to be employed in the transport and glider tug roles in almost all the major airborne assault operations by the RAF in the last two years of the war.

Specification:
Armstrong Whitworth Albemarle Mk I
Type: four-crew transport/glider tug
Powerplant: two 1,590-hp (1186-kW) Bristol Hercules XI radial pistons
Performance: max speed 265 mph (426 km/h) at 10,500 ft (3200 m); initial climb rate 980 ft (299 m) per minute; service ceiling 18,000 ft (5485 m); range 1,300 miles (2092 km)
Weights: empty 21,800 lb (9888 kg); max take-off 36,500 lb (16556 kg)
Dimensions: span 17 ft 0 in (23.47 m); length 59 ft 11 in (1826 m); height 15 ft 7 in (4.75 m); wing area 803.5 sq ft (74.65 m²)
Armament: two 0.303-in (7 7-mm) machine-guns in dorsal turret
Accommodation: up to 12 fully-armed paratroops

Armstrong Whitworth Whitley

Withdrawn from Bomber Command when the emphasis shifted to four-engined bombers, the Whitley continued to serve with Coastal Command. The Whitley Mk VII shown here belonged to No. 502 (Ulster) Sqn, at Holmsley South in 1943.

Rugged workhorse of RAF Bomber Command at the start of the war, the twin-engined **Armstrong Whitworth Whitley** had been designed to a 1934 requirement and first flew on 4 June 1935. The Whitley **Mk I** (Tiger IX radial engines) and Whitley **Mk II** (Tiger VIII) had been largely relegated to training duties by September 1939, and Merlin X-powered Whitley **Mk V**s were being delivered to the RAF, remaining in production from 1939 until 1943. A total of 1,476 was built.

Whitleys carried out the majority of the controversial leaflet raids during the first year of the war and joined in Bomber Command's night offensive over Europe from 1940, making their last raid (on Ostend) on 29-30 April 1942. Whitley Mk Vs of Nos 51 and 78 Squadrons took part in the first RAF raid on Berlin of 25/26 August 1940. The Whitley Mk V was used in early paratroop attacks on the Italian viaduct at Tragino on 10 February 1941 and in the Bruneval raid of 27/28 February 1942. The type was also used as a glider tug for the Airspeed Horsa glider.

The Whitley **Mk VII** served with RAF Coastal Command, entering service in March 1941 for anti-submarine duties over the Atlantic; aircraft of No. 502 Squadron were the first to be equipped with the long-range ASV Mk II radar, and achieved the first U-boat kill with ASV when U-206 was sunk in the Bay of Biscay on 30 November 1941.

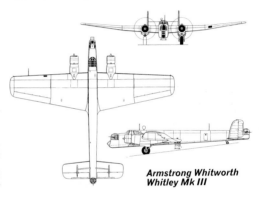

Armstrong Whitworth Whitley Mk III

Specification:
Armstrong Whitworth Whitley Mk V
Type: five-crew long-range heavy bomber
Powerplant: two 1,145-hp (854-kW) Rolls-Royce Merlin X inline pistons
Performance: max speed 222 mph (357km/h) at 7000 ft (5180 m); initial climb rate 800 ft (244 m) per minute; ceiling 17,600 ft (5365 m); range 1,650 miles (2655 km) with 3,000-lb (1361-kg) load
Weights: empty 19,330 lb (8768 kg); max take-off 33,500 lb (15196 kg)
Dimensions: span 84 ft 0 in (25.60 m); length 69 ft 3 in (21.11 m); height 15 ft 0 in (4.57 m); wing area 1,137.0 sq ft (105.63 m²)
Armament: 0.303-in (7.7-mm) gun in nose and tail turret; max bomb load 7,000 lb (3175 kg), usually 14 of 500 lb (227 kg) each

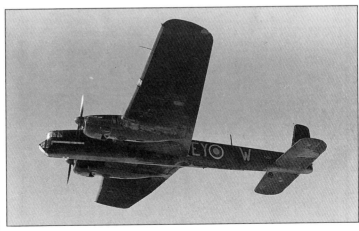

The Whitley bomber was immensely rugged and, despite a somewhat sluggish performance, was widely used by RAF Bomber Command during the first two years of the war, particularly in the often criticised leaflet 'raids' over Germany in the first months.

Avro Anson

Representative of the Ansons which undertook anti-submarine patrols over the North Sea from the first days of the war is this Mk I of No. 206 Sqn based at Manston. Ansons served on no fewer than 57 RAF squadrons.

Anachronistic relic of pre-war RAF expansion, the **Anson** was the result of a coastal reconnaissance aircraft requirement, and was developed from a six-seat commercial aircraft. It first flew on 24 March 1935 and, powered by Cheetah engines, the **Mk I** entered service with No. 48 Squadron in March 1936. It was the first RAF aircraft with a retractable landing gear, albeit manually operated. The Anson served with 12 squadrons of Coastal Command up to the beginning of the war, when the first Lockheed Hudsons began to arrive from America. Ansons were retained on short-range coastal reconnaissance duties in diminishing numbers until 1942, occasionally having brushes with the enemy. By 1939, the Anson was in use as an aircrew trainer for navigators, wireless operators and air gunners, and it was for this service that the 'faithful Annie' is best remembered. Jacobs- and Wright-powered Anson **Mks III** and **IV** aircraft were shipped to Canada to equip the growing numbers of flying schools under the Commonwealth Air Training Scheme, Canadian manufacturers also producing the Anson **Mks II**, **V** and **VI**. Light transport conversions from the Anson Mk I resulted in the

Anson **Mks X**, **XI** and **XII**, some of which were employed as air ambulances. The Anson Mk XI was powered by Cheetah XIX engines driving Fairey-Reed metal propellers, and the Anson Mk XII had Cheetah XVs driving constant-speed Rotol propellers. Production, which continued after the war with the Anson **Mks 19**, **20**, **21** and **22**, reached a total of 11,020 aircraft (2,882 built in Canada).

Avro Anson Mk X

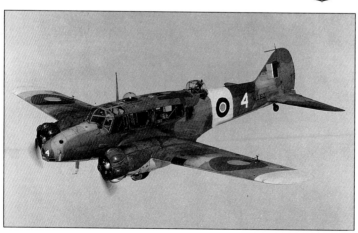

Serving as a coastal patrol aircraft at the beginning of the war, the Anson was quickly replaced by the Lockheed Hudson, and was then used almost exclusively as a trainer. A late production Anson Mk I is pictured here.

Specification: Avro Anson Mk 1
Type: three-crew general-reconnaissance aircraft
Powerplant: two 350-hp (261-kW) Armstrong Siddeley Cheetah IX radial pistons
Performance: max speed 188 mph (302 km/h) at 7,000 ft (2135 m); initial climb rate 720 ft (219 m) per minute; service ceiling 19,000 ft (5790 m); range 790 miles (1271 km)
Weights: empty 5,375 lb (2438 kg); max take-off 8,000 lb (3629 kg)
Dimensions: span 56 ft 6 in (17.22 m); length 42 ft 3 in (1287 m); height 13 ft 1 in (3.99 m); wing area 463.0 sq ft (43.01 m²)
Armament: one 0.303-in (7.7-mm) machine-gun in nose, one 0.303-in (7.7-mm) machine-gun in dorsal turret; provision for 360 lb (163 kg) of bombs

Avro Lancaster

In order to carry the 22,000-lb (9976-kg) 'Grand Slam' bomb, the Lancaster B.Mk I (Special) had two turrets removed and a cut-away fuselage. The bombs were dropped on the Bielefeld viaduct by No. 617 Sqn.

Undisputably the finest night heavy bomber of the war, the four-engined **Lancaster** was developed when the two-Vulture Manchester proved to be a failure on account of its engines. Roy Chadwick substituted four Rolls-Royce Merlins in the new bomber, which flew on 9 January 1941, the first RAF squadron (No. 44) being completely equipped with Lancaster **Mk I**s (of which 3,544 were built) in January 1942. The type's first bombing raid was carried out on Essen on 10-11 March that year; one month later, Lancasters dropped the first 8,000-lb (3629-kg) bomb (also on Essen) and followed with the first 12,000-lb (5443-kg) bomb on 15-16 September 1943, and the first 22,000-lb (9979-kg) bomb on 14 March 1945. The Lancaster **Mk II** (of which 300 were built) was powered by 1,650-hp (1231-kW) Bristol Hercules VI radials and the **Mk III** (2,990 built) by Packard-built Merlin 28, 38 or 224 engines. These versions came to constitute Bomber Command's main force equipment, being fitted with Gee, H2S and all manner of other navigation and bombing radar aids. Lancaster **Mk I (Special)** aircraft were adapted to carry the special mines used in the famous dams raid by No. 617

Squadron. Later wartime versions included the **Mk VI** with Merlin 87s driving four-bladed propellers, the Lancaster **Mk I (FE)** prepared for Far Eastern service, and the Lancaster **Mk VII** (built by Austin) with revised dorsal turret. Total Lancaster production was 7,366 (422 Mk Xs built in Canada). Lancasters dropped 608,612 tons of bombs and flew 156,000 sorties during the war.

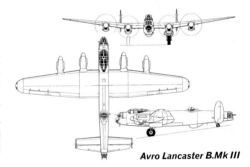

Avro Lancaster B.Mk III

Specification: Avro Lancaster Mk I
Type: seven-crew bomber
Powerplant: four 1,460-hp (1089-kW) Rolls-Royce Merlin XX inline pistons
Performance: max speed 287 mph (462 km/h) at 11,500 ft (3505 m); climb to 20,000 ft (6095 m) in 41.6 minutes; service ceiling 24,500 ft (7470 m); range with 14,000-lb (6350-kg) load 660 miles (2671 km)
Weights: empty 36,900 lb (16738 kg); max take-off with 14,000 lb (6350 kg) of bombs 68,000 lb (30845 kg)
Dimensions: span 102 ft 0 in (31.09 m); length 69 ft 6 in (21.18 m); height 20 ft 0 in (6.10 m); wing area 1,297.0 sq ft (120.49 m²)
Armament: two 0.303-in (7.7-mm) guns in nose, dorsal & ventral turrets, four 0.303-in (7.7-mm) guns in tail turret; 14 1,000-lb (454-kg) bombs

Most famous night-bomber of all time, the Lancaster served with a total of 65 squadrons of the RAF, and eventually carried the heaviest bomb dropped by aircraft in the war, the 22,000-lb (9976-kg) 'Grand Slam'. A Merlin-powered Lancaster Mk I is shown.

Bell P-39 Airacobra

No fewer than 4,924 P-39Ns and P-39Os were shipped to the USSR, many over the Alaska-Siberia route from America. Soviet P-39 pilots Captain Grigori A. Rechkalov of the 9th Guards Fighter Division achieved 44 victories with P-39s, out of a total of 58.

The radical **P-39** single-seat fighter was designed around the 37-mm T-9 cannon which had given impressive demonstrations in 1935. The hub-firing arrangement of this gun dictated the midship location of the Allison inline engine behind the cockpit, driving the propeller by an extension shaft; this in turn led to adoption of a nosewheel landing gear. The prototype **XP-39** was first flown in April 1939. Production **P-39D**s entered service with the USAAC in 1941 and first saw combat in the Pacific theatre in April 1942. P-39Ds also served with US forces in Europe but suffered heavily in action. They flew with one RAF squadron (No. 601) but persistent problems caused them to be withdrawn after scarcely a single action. The Airacobra had much better results flying with three USAAF groups based in North Africa from the end of 1942. The P-39D was followed by the P-39F, which introduced an Aeroproducts propeller in place of the former Curtiss type, the **P-39J** with V-1710-59 engine, the **P-39K** with -63 engine and Aeroproducts propeller, and the **P-39L** with -63 engine and Curtiss propeller. The **P-39M** introduced the -83 engine with larger-diameter propeller. The final and most-

built versions were the **P-39N** and **P-39Q** with -85 engine; production amounted to 2,095, bringing the total of all P-39s to 9,558. Of these, 4,773 were shipped to the Soviet Union in response to Stalin's desperate appeals for military assistance.

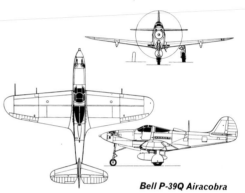

Bell P-39Q Airacobra

Although fast and heavily armed, the Airacobra never achieved the popularity of its contemporary trio – the P-38, P-47 and P-51 – among the Western Allies. It was somewhat tricky to fly and unforgiving of handling mistakes, particularly during landing.

Specification: Bell P-39N Airacobra
Type: single-seat interceptor fighter
Powerplant: one 1,200-hp (895-kW) Allison V-1710-85 inline piston
Performance: max speed 399 mph (642 km/h) at 9,700 ft (2955 m); climb to 15,000 ft (4570 m) in 3.8 minutes; service ceiling 38,500 ft (11735 m): range 750 miles (1207 km)
Weights: empty 5,657 lb (2566 kg); max take-off 8,200 lb (3720 kg)
Dimensions: span 34 ft 0 in (10.36 m) length 30 ft 2 in (9.19 m); height 12 ft 5 in (3.78 m); wing area 213.0 sq ft (19.79 m²)
Armament: one hub-firing 37-mm gun, two 0.5-in (12.7-mm) guns in nose decking, four 0.3-in (7.62-mm) guns in wings; one 500-lb (227-kg) bomb under the fuselage

Blackburn Skua

Originally conceived as a dive-bomber, suitable targets for the Skua were rare and it served in an ad hoc capacity. Sometimes used as a fleet fighter, its wing armament of four machine-guns was in theory no lighter than that of the Sea Gladiator.

Occupying a niche unique in British naval aviation, the **Blackburn Skua** was a two-seat fighter dive-bomber which gave valuable service in the first two years of the war. Designed to a 1934 specification, the prototype Skua first flew on 9 February 1937, being powered by an 840-hp (627-kW) Bristol Mercury IX radial. This and a second aircraft were termed Skua **Mk I**s, but the production aircraft were Skua **Mk II**s with 890-hp (664-kW) Perseus XIIs. By the outbreak of war 154 of the 190 aircraft on order had been delivered and were serving with Nos 800, 801, 803 and 806 Squadrons. It was a Skua, flown by Lieutenant B. S. McEwen RN of No. 803 Squadron from HMS *Ark Royal*, which shot down the first German aircraft to fall to British aircraft guns (a Dornier Do 18 over the North Sea on 25 September 1939). During the Norwegian campaign, Skuas of Nos 800 and 803 Squadrons flew from Hatston in the Orkneys to Bergen, where they dive-bombed and sank the German cruiser *Konigsberg* on 10 April 1940. Skuas of No. 801 Squadron took part in the defence of Dunkirk during the famous evacuation, while others from *Ark Royal* attacked the French

fleet in Oran harbour in September 1940. Skuas remained in front-line service until August 1941, when they were replaced by Fulmars and Sea Hurricanes, and were relegated to training and target-towing duties. Similar to the Skua was the **Blackburn Roc** turret fighter (136 produced).

Blackburn Skua Mk II

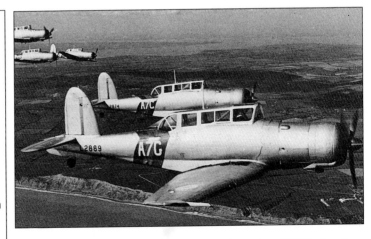

The Fleet Air Arm's Blackburn Skua served aboard a number of British aircraft-carriers at the beginning of the war and gave good service, particularly over the North Sea; during the Norwegian campaign of 1940 it operated from airfields ashore to protect the British Expeditionary Force.

Specification:
Blackburn Skua Mk II
Type: two-seat shipborne fighter/dive-bomber
Powerplant: one 890-hp (664-kW) Bristol Perseus XII radial piston
Performance: max speed 225 mph (362 km/h) at 6,500 ft (1980 m); initial climb rate 1,580 ft (482 m) per minute; service ceiling 20,200 ft (6155 m); range 435 miles (700 km)
Weights: empty 5,496 lb (2493 kg); max take-off 8,228 lb (3732 kg)
Dimensions: span 46 ft 2 in (14.07 m); length 35 ft 7 in (10.84 m); height 12 ft 6 in (3.81 m); wing area 319.0 sq ft (29.64 m²)
Armament: four 0.303-in (7.7-mm) machine-guns in the wings and one in the rear cockpit; one 500-lb (227-kg) bomb

Bloch 151/152/155

Despite its ability to survive much greater battle damage than other French fighters of 1940, the Bloch 152 nevertheless suffered the heaviest casualties; of the 632 aircraft taken on charge, about 270 were lost to enemy action in the Battle of France.

Outmoded and handicapped by a radial engine of inadequate power, the **Bloch 151** series single-seat fighters constituted the bulk of French fighter resistance during the Battle of France in 1940. Nevertheless, they packed a powerful punch and, flown with skill and bravery, inflicted surprisingly heavy casualties on the Luftwaffe. Like so many wartime French aircraft, the Bloch 150 had stemmed from a 1934 requirement, but the proto-type **M.B.150-01** failed to leave the ground for its first flight on 17 July 1936. Development contin-ued, however, and after a successful flight by the **M.B.150-01M** on 29 September 1937, the type eventually entered production as the **M.B.151** with Gnome-Rhône 14 N 35 radial engines, and the **M.B.152** with 14 N 25 and 49 engines. By mid-January 1940, the Armée de l'Air had received 138 M.B.151s and 274 M.B.152s, but many were still without essential components. The situation had improved by the time of the German attack in the west, when the number of M.B.152s had risen to 363 in service with five *groupes de chasse*. A new variant, the **M.B.155** with two additional 7.5-mm (0.295-in) guns, started delivery just before the

armistice, but only a few were flown during the Battle of France. Against the combat loss of 270 M.B.151s and M.B.152s during May and June 1940, their pilots destroyed 146 German aircraft. Total production of the M.B.151 and M.B.152 amounted to 593.

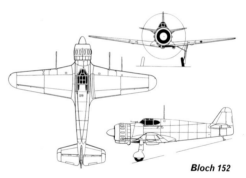

Bloch 152

Typifying the nature of operations flown by the French fighters was that during 3 June 1940, when 300 bombers attacked the Paris area; the M.B.152s were caught by Messerschmitt Bf 109Es and four German aircraft were shot down for the loss of nine M.B.152s, with three more damaged.

Specification:
Bloch 152
Type: single-seat fighter
Powerplant: one 870-hp (649-kW) Gnome-Rhône 14 N 25 radial piston
Performance: max speed 299 mph (482 km/h) at 16,405 ft (5000 m); climb to 16,405 ft (5000 m) in 60 minutes; service ceiling 32,810 ft (10000 m); range 581 miles (935 km)
Weights: empty 4,453 lb (2020 kg); normal loaded 5,842 lb (2650 kg)
Dimensions: span 34 ft 5⅜ in (10.50 m); length 29 ft 10¼ in (9.10 m); height 9 ft 11½ in (3.03 m); wing area 186.4 sq ft (17.32 m²)
Armament: two 20-mm HS 404 cannon and two 7.5-mm (0.295-in) MAC 1934 machine-guns

Boeing B-17 Fortress

This Boeing B-17F-10 BO belonged to the 322nd Squadron of the 91st Bomb Group based at Bassingbourn, Cambs, under the 1st Bombardment Wing. This aircraft did not return from the Stuttgart mission of 6 September 1943.

The US Army Air Corps issued in 1934 a requirement for high-flying, heavily-armed bombers for which the Boeing Model 299 was designed and first flown on 28 July 1935. Twelve **YB-17**s entered service in 1937 and were followed by small numbers of **B-17B**s and **B-17C**s in 1940-41, and by the **B-17D** in 1941. The **B-17E** (512 built) introduced the enlarged vertical tail surfaces and tail gun position characteristic of all subsequent B-17s, as well as power-operated twin gun turrets aft of the cockpit and below the centre fuselage. This version was the first USAAF heavy bomber to see combat in Europe with the 8th Air Force. A total of 3,400 **B-17F**s, with enlarged one-piece nose transparency, was produced during 1942-43. These were followed by the **B-17G**, which, in reply to calls for improved nose armament to counter head-on attacks, introduced the two-gun 'chin' turret; production totalled 8,685 aircraft by Boeing, Douglas and Lockheed-Vega. The Fortress was deployed principally in Europe during the war, with smaller numbers in the Far East. They carried out daylight raids in which large formations of bombers, providing mutual protection against enemy fighters,

pounded across the skies over Germany. Heavy losses later forced the Americans to introduce escort fighters – the P-38, P-47 and P-51. One expedient involved the use of a small number of B-17s modified as **YB-40** 'escort' aircraft, some aircraft carrying up to 30 machine-guns. Fortresses (B-17Ds and B-17Fs) also served in small numbers with RAF Bomber and Coastal Commands.

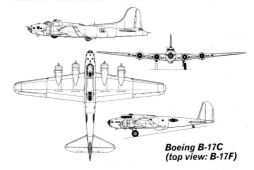

Boeing B-17C (top view: B-17F)

Specification: Boeing B-17G Flying Fortress
Type: 10-crew daylight medium/heavy bomber
Powerplant: four 1,200-hp (895-kW) Wright Cyclone R-1820-97 radial pistons
Performance: max speed 287 mph (462 km/h) at 25,000 ft (7620 m); climb to 20,000 ft (6095 m) in 37.0 minutes; service ceiling 35,600 ft (10850 m); range with 6,000-lb (2722-kg) load 2,000 miles (3219 km)
Weights: empty 36,135 lb (16391 kg); max take-off 72,000 lb (32660 kg)
Dimensions: span 103 ft 9 in (31.62 m); length 74 ft 9 in (22.78 m); height 19 ft 1 in (5.82m); wing area 1,420.0 sq ft (131.92 m²)
Armament: 0.5-in (12.7-mm) gun under nose, aft of cockpit, under fuselage, in tail, nose sides, radio op's hatch, waist; max bombs 17,600 lb (7983 kg)

Formation and low-level training over southern England was undertaken on 'down' days. Tight formation allowed mutual defence from the B-17's many guns. These B-17s are from the 447th Bomb Group.

Boeing B-29 Superfortress

The B-29's remotely-controlled turrets were periscopically sighted by gunners located within the fuselage. The aircraft illustrated, carrying BTO (bombing through overcast) radar, was based on Tinian for the final raids on Japan.

Design of the **B-29** heavy bomber started in 1940 to meet a US Army Air Corps requirement for a 'Hemisphere Defense Weapon', an aircraft capable of carrying 2,000 lb (907 kg) of bombs for 5,333 miles (8582 km) at 400 mph (644 km/h). Only after the Japanese attack on Pearl Harbor was the project given top priority, and the first **XB-29** was flown on 21 September 1942. The four-engined mid-wing bomber had by then been ordered in large numbers, and in 1943 the decision was taken to deploy the B-29 only against Japan, concentrating them in the XX Bomber Command on bases in India and China. The first **YB-29**s were delivered to the 58th Bomb Wing in July 1943, followed by **B-29-BW**s three months later. Production was concentrated at Boeing Wichita, Bell Atlanta, Martin Omaha, and a Boeing-run factory at Renton. Four groups of B-29s moved to India early in 1944, making their first raid on Bangkok on 5 June and on the Japanese mainland 10 days later. For the first nine months the B-29s were employed in high-level daylight raids, but on 9 March 1945 they switched to low-level night attacks with devastating incendiary raids on Japanese cities (the first, on Tokyo, killed

80,000). The **B-29A-BN** featured four-gun forward upper turret and increased wingspan, and the **B-29B-BA** had reduced gun armament and increased bomb load. **B-29-45-MO**s 'Enola Gay' and 'Bock's Car' of the 393rd Bomb Sqn dropped the atomic bombs 'Little Boy' and 'Fat Boy' on Hiroshima and Nagasaki on 6 and 9 August 1945, respectively. Total B-29 production was 3,970.

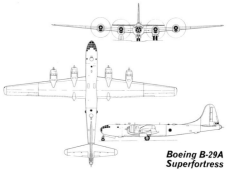

Boeing B-29A Superfortress

The mighty Superfortress. One of the most remarkable achievements of the war was the design, development and production of this bomber in the space of four years. All B-29s were assigned to the assault on Japan, the two aircraft seen here – YB-29s – being flown by the 58th Bomb Wing (Very Heavy).

Specification: Boeing B-29A Superfortress
Type: 10-crew heavy bomber
Powerplant: four 2,200-hp (1641-kW) Wright R-3350-57 radial pistons
Performance: max speed 358 mph (576 km/h) at 25,000 ft (7620 m); climb to 20,000 ft (6095 m) in 38 minutes; ceiling 31,800 ft (9695 m); range 4,100 miles (6598 km)
Weights: empty 71,360 lb (32369 kg); max take-off 141,100 lb (64003 kg)
Dimensions: span 142 ft 3 in (43.36 m); length 99 ft 0 in (30.18 m); height 29 ft 7 in (9.01 m); wing area 1,736.0 sq ft (161 27 m²)
Armament: four-gun turret over nose, two-gun turrets under nose, under and over rear fuselage, all of 0.5-in (12.7-mm) calibre, and one 20-mm and two 0.5-in (12.7-mm) guns in tail; max bombs 20,000 lb (9072 kg)

Boulton Paul Defiant

This Defiant wears the markings of No. 264 Sqn, the pennant below the cockpit denoting the aircraft of the CO, Squadron Leader P. A. Hunter, who was killed on 24 August 1940 in the Battle of Britain. The Defiant was transferred to night-fighting.

The **Defiant** was schemed in 1937 as the smallest aircraft able to accept a two-man crew, a single Merlin inline engine and a four-gun power-operated turret (located close to the centre of gravity) capable of heavy fire towards the flanks of the aircraft. The prototype Defiant was first flown on 11 August 1937, and the type joined No. 264 Squadron in December 1939. Powered by a 1,030-hp (768-kW) Merlin III inline engine, the **Mk I** was armed with four 0.303-in (7.7-mm) Browning machine-guns in the dorsal turret, but was totally devoid of fixed forward-firing armament, and the turret could not be trained to fire directly forwards. The fighter was flown with some success during the Dunkirk evacuation, German pilots being misled by the type's superficial resemblance to 'conventional' single-seat fighters, but during the Battle of Britain Nos 141 and 264 Squadrons suffered disastrous losses to German pilots then aware of the type's armament and performance limitations. The Defiant was retasked with night-fighting, a role for which it was better suited. Defiant Mk I aircraft at first operated 'blind', but **Mk IA** aircraft had AI.Mk IV or Mk VI radar. The **Mk II** – a day fighter with the 1,260-hp (940-kW) Merlin XX – was already in service, and was rapidly converted into a night-fighter. Other roles undertaken by the Defiant were air-sea rescue, radar calibration and countermeasures and (in the **Mk III** produced by conversion of Mk Is) target-towing. Production ceased in February 1943 after the building of 1,060 Defiants.

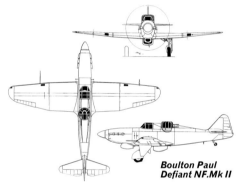

Boulton Paul Defiant NF.Mk II

Specification: Boulton Paul Defiant Mk II
Type: two-seat night-fighter
Powerplant: one 1,260-hp (940-kW) Rolls-Royce Merlin XX inline piston
Performance: max speed 315 mph (507 km/h) at 16,500 ft (5030 m); initial climb rate 2,050 ft (625 m) per minute; service ceiling 31,800 ft (9690 m); range 480 miles (772 km)
Weights: empty 6,150 lb (2892 kg); max take-off 8,600 lb (3901 kg)
Dimensions: span 39 ft 4 in (11.99 m); length 35 ft 4 in (10.77 m); height 12 ft 2 in (3.71 m); wing area 250.0 sq ft (23.23 m²)
Armament: four 0.303-in (7.7-mm) Browning machine-guns in dorsal turret

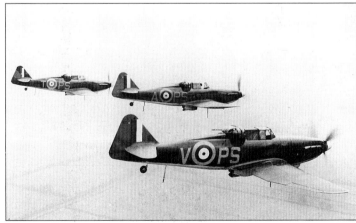

Designed as a two-seat interceptor fighter armed only with a four-gun power-operated turret, the Defiant had a brief moment of glory over Dunkirk, but the two squadrons which were committed in the Battle of Britain were decimated by German single-seat fighters.

Brewster F2A Buffalo

This B-339D (export version of the Buffalo) belonged to 1 Afdeling, Vliegtuiggroep V. ML-KNIL of the Royal Netherlands Indies Army Air Corps. It was based at Semplak, Java, in the summer of 1941.

The first monoplane fighter to enter operational service with the US Navy, the **Buffalo** first flew as the **XF2A-1** prototype in December 1937. The **F2A-1** initial production version became operational with VF-3 aboard the USS *Saratoga* in June 1940, the 11 aircraft being powered by the 940-hp (701-kW) R-1820-34 radial. The **F2A-2** followed, with redesigned vertical tail surfaces and the uprated 1,200-hp (895-kW) R-1820-40. The 43 F2A-2s were followed by 108 **F2A-3**s with some armour protection and lengthened nose, but otherwise similar to the F2A-2. These 162 aircraft comprised the entire F2A production for the US services, and the type saw limited combat use, largely with the USMC's VMF-221 in the Battle of Midway in 1942. Export aircraft included the **B-239** version of the F2A-1, 44 of which were built against a Finnish order. The **B-339** was produced in the **B-339B** and **B-339D** versions (40 and 72, respectively) against Belgian and Dutch orders. The two versions were essentially land-based variants of the F2A-1. Thirty-eight of the Belgian order were diverted to the UK, which also accepted 170 **B-339E**s as **Buffalo Mk I**. Final production version was the **B-439**, an export

version of the F2A-3. All 20 (ordered by the Netherlands for service in the Dutch East Indies) were delivered to the USAAF, which later passed 17 to Australia. The Buffaloes were unsuited to European operations – although the Finns enjoyed success against the Russians – and most export aircraft served in the Far East, suffering defeat over Malaya, Burma and the Dutch East Indies.

Brewster F2A-3 Buffalo

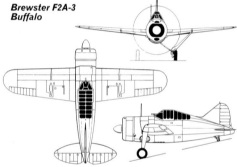

First monoplane fighter to serve with a US Navy squadron, the F2A Buffalo was already obsolete when America entered the war. It suffered heavy casualties in its only major Pacific combat with the US Marine Corps, the great Battle of Midway.

Specification:
Brewster F2A-3
Type: single-seat shipboard fighter
Powerplant: one 1,200-hp (895-kW) Wright R-1820-40 radial piston
Performance: max speed 321 mph (516 km/h) at 16,500 ft (5030 m); initial climb rate 2,290 m (698 m) per minute; service ceiling 32,300 ft (10120 m); max range 965 miles (1650 km)
Weights: empty 4,732 lb (2146 kg); max take-off 7,159 lb (3247 kg)
Dimensions: span 35 ft 0 in (1067 m); length 26 ft 4 in (802 m); height 12 ft 1 in (368 m); wing area 208.9 sq ft (1941 m²)
Armament: four 0.5-in (12.7-mm) Browning machine-guns, two in nose and two in wings

Bristol Beaufighter

This early Beaufighter TF.Mk X of No. 455 Sqn, RAF, is equipped for anti-shipping strike duties with eight underwing rockets. Rocket- and torpedo-equipped Beaufighters served together in special anti-shipping strike wings.

The RAF's first purpose-built night-fighter, the twin-engined **Beaufighter** initially arrived in service in small numbers at the beginning of the German night Blitz in September 1940, having first flown on 17 July 1939. The Beaufighter **Mk I** with Bristol Hercules radials was produced in two forms: **Mk IF** for Fighter Command and **Mk IC** for Coastal Command. The former, equipped with AI.Mk IV radar, gained its first confirmed night victory on 19 November 1940. The **Mk IIF** followed, powered with two Rolls-Royce Merlin XX inline engines. It joined home-based night-fighter squadrons in 1941, by which time the heavily-armed fighter was taking a respectable toll on enemy night raiders. The **Mk VI**, also produced in **Mk VIF** and **Mk VIC** versions, reverted to Hercules radials, but of increased power, and the Mk VIC introduced a Vickers gun to fire aft from the navigator's hatch. By 1942, Beaufighters were flying with a sharply dihedralled tailplane, and the Mk VI also introduced an extended dorsal fin to counter take-off swing. Underwing rockets and an 18-in (457-mm) torpedo were carried by some Mk VICs. As the Mosquito had assumed the night-fighting role,

the definitive ASV-equipped **TF.Mk X** was delivered to Coastal Command as a long-range strike fighter, employing torpedo, rockets, bombs and guns. Beaufighters served in the Mediterranean, and in the Far East performed very well against the Japanese in Burma. Production of the Beaufighter (also undertaken in Australia) continued until September 1945, with 5,562 aircraft produced.

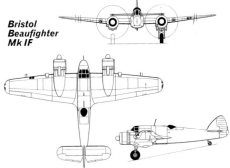

Bristol Beaufighter Mk IF

Specification: Bristol Beaufighter Mk VIF
Type: two-seat night-fighter
Powerplant: two 1,670-hp (1246-kW) Bristol Hercules VI or XVI radial pistons
Performance: max speed 333 mph (536 km/h) at 15,600 ft (4755 m); climb to 15,000 ft (4570 m) in 7.8 minutes; service ceiling 26,500 ft (8075 m); range 1,480 miles (2382 km)
Weights: empty 14,600 lb (6623 kg); max take-off 21,600 lb (9798 kg)
Dimensions: span 57 ft 10 in (17.63 m); length 41 ft 8 in (12.70 m); height 15 ft 10 in (4.82 m); wing area 5030 sq ft (46.73 m²)
Armament: four 20-mm cannon in nose, two 0.303-in (7.7-mm) machine-guns in port wing, four 0.303-in (7.7 mm) machine-guns in starboard wing

The Beaufighter was the RAF's first purpose-designed night-fighter and pioneered the science of radar-directed interception. Powerful and heavily-armed, the aircraft served on almost every front during the war in a variety of roles and gained a fine reputation in the Mediterranean and Far East.

Bristol Beaufort

This Beaufort Mk I wears the markings of No. 22 Sqn. Flying Officer K. Campbell of this squadron, in a Beaufort, carried out a torpedo attack on German warships in Brest harbour, scoring a direct hit on the Gneisenau.

Until superseded by the torpedo-carrying Beaufighter, the **Beaufort** was the RAF's standard torpedo-bomber from 1940 to 1943, replacing the aged Vickers Vildebeest biplane. First flown on 15 October 1938, the Beaufort **Mk I**, of which early versions were powered by 1,010-hp (753-kW) Bristol Taurus II radials (subsequently replaced by Taurus VIs), joined No. 22 Squadron in December 1939 and carried out their first minelaying sortie on 15-16 August 1940. Beauforts also dropped the RAF's first 2,000-lb (907-kg) bomb on 7 May. This version was followed by the Beaufort **Mk II** with American Pratt & Whitney Twin Wasp radials, production continuing until 1943, by which time 415 had been produced. The final Beaufort Mk IIs were completed as trainers with the two-gun dorsal turret deleted. Beauforts equipped six Coastal Command squadrons in the United Kingdom and four in the Middle East, their most famous operations being carried out against the German warships *Scharnhorst* and *Gneisenau* on 6 April 1941 in Brest harbour (which earned a posthumous VC for Flying Officer Kenneth Campbell of No. 22 Squadron), and during the warships' escape up the

English Channel early in 1942. Beauforts were also very active while based on Malta, attacking Axis shipping en route to North Africa. The Beaufort **Mks V-IX** were built in Australia for the RAAF in the Far East, production totalling 700.

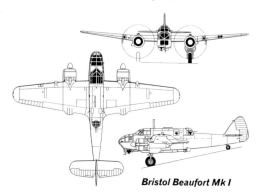

Bristol Beaufort Mk I

These two Bristol Beaufort Mk Is with Taurus radial engines are from No. 42 Squadron, Royal Air Force, and are seen flying in formation. A total of 965 examples of this version was produced.

Specification: Bristol Beaufort Mk I
Type: four-crew torpedo-bomber
Powerplant: two 1,130-hp (843-kW) Bristol Taurus VI radials
Performance: max speed 265 mph (426 km/h) at 6,000 ft (1830 m); service ceiling 16,500 ft (5030 m); range 1,600 miles (2574 km)
Weights: empty 13,100 lb (5942 kg); max take-off 21,228 lb (9629 kg)
Dimensions: span 57 ft 10 in (17.62 m); length 44 ft 3 in (13.49 m); height 14 ft 3 in (4.34 m); wing area 503.0 sq ft (46.73 m²)
Armament: two 0.303-in (7.7-mm) guns in nose and dorsal turret (some with rear-firing gun under nose and two in beam-firing positions); bomb load 2,000 lb (907 kg) or one 1,605-lb (728-kg) 18-in (457-mm) torpedo

Bristol Blenheim

The Blenheim Mk IV gave steadfast service well into the war, spearheading the British day bomber force in the first two years. The aircraft shown served with LeLv 42 of the Finnish air force late in 1942, at the onset of the Continuation War.

At the beginning of the war the RAF's principal twin-engined light bomber was the **Blenheim**, the aircraft having first entered service in its **Mk I** form with No. 114 Squadron in March 1937. Capable of outpacing the then-current RAF biplane fighters, the Mk I was being replaced by the **Mk IV** as a home-based bomber in 1939, the latter featuring a longer nose with conventional 'stepped' cockpit windscreen. The short-nose **Mk IF** continued in service throughout 1940 as a night-fighter with Fighter Command, however, having been fitted with a tray of four 0.303-in (7.7 mm) machine-guns under the fuselage; some of these aircraft pioneered the RAF's first airborne interception radar, gaining the world's first night AI victory on 22 July 1940. Bomber Command's Mk IVs continued in service for three years, making many memorable raids during that time, their last operation being flown on 18 August 1942. This version also served with Coastal Command, both as a fighter (the **Mk IVF**) and as an anti-shipping bomber, and in a period of six months in 1941 sank 70 enemy ships. Blenheim Mk IVs flew with the RAF in the Mediterranean and Middle East until 1943, and in the Far East participated in the defence of Singapore and in the Burma campaign. The **Mk V** with Mercury XXX – the principal version of which was the tropicalised **Mk VD** – entered service in North Africa at the end of 1942, but was too slow and vulnerable and was soon withdrawn. A total of about 4,440 Blenheims was produced.

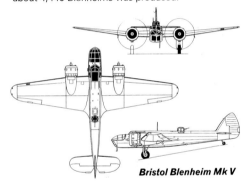

Bristol Blenheim Mk V

Specification: Bristol Blenheim Mk IV
Type: three-crew light bomber
Powerplant: two 920-hp (686-kW) Bristol Mercury XV radial pistons
Performance: max speed 266 mph (423 km/h) at 11,800 ft (3595 m); initial climb rate 1,500 ft (457 m) per minute; service ceiling 22,000 ft (6705 m); range 1,460 miles (2350 km)
Weights: empty 9,790 lb (4441 kg); max take-off 13,500 lb (6124 kg)
Dimensions: span 56 ft 4 in (17.17 m); length 42 ft 7 in (12.98 m); height 9 ft 10 in (2.99 m); wing area 469.0 sq ft (43.57 m²)
Armament: one fixed forward-firing 0.303-in (7.7-mm) gun in nose, two 0.303-in (7.7-mm) guns in dorsal turret; bomb load 1,000 lb (454 kg) internally, 320 lb (145 kg) externally

Obsolescent at the outbreak of war, the Blenheim Mk I nevertheless continued to serve as a night-fighter. This radar-equipped Mk IF with four-gun pack under the fuselage flew with No. 54 Operational Training Unit.

Cant Z.1007 Alcione

Built largely of wood, the attractive Cant Z.1007 had a creditable performance. However, like so many Italian aircraft, the defensive armament was poor and many Airone (Heron) bombers fell to equally mediocre British fighters.

Product of Cantieri Riuniti dell'Adriatico ('Cant') – synonymous since the mid-1920s with Italian flying-boats and floatplanes – the **Z.1007 Alcione** (Kingfisher) was a logical development of the Z.506B Airone (Heron) floatplane, itself a military counterpart of the commercial Z.506A. The prototype, with three 840-hp (627-kW) Isotta Fraschini Asso engines, was first flown in May 1937 and gained a favourable response from test establishments. Early production aircraft were armed with four 7.7-mm (0.303-in) machine-guns in dorsal turret, beam hatches and ventral position, but later Alciones had 12.7-mm (0.5-in) guns in the turret and ventral position. Production got under way in 1939 and the first aircraft joined the Regia Aeronautica later that year. The main production version, the **Z.1007bis**, was powered by three 1,000-hp (746-kW) Piaggio radials, and featured a larger fuselage, increased wing area and strengthened landing gear; most aircraft also changed to a twin-finned tail unit. Z.1007s were used in the torpedo-bombing role, particularly in operations against the Malta convoys, but were mainly employed in night-bombing operations over the

Aegean, Malta and North Africa. Its weak gun defence rendered the Z.1007 vulnerable to mid-war Allied fighters, yet the type saw service until September 1943, some serving on the Russian Front. The metal-construction, twin-engined **Z.1018 Leone** (Lion) was developed from the Alcione, but scarcely entered service before Italy surrendered.

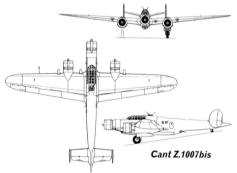

Cant Z.1007bis

The big all-wood Cant Z.1007 tri-motor bomber was produced in both single- and twin-fin versions and served side-by-side on the same squadrons. These aircraft are from the 230ª Squadriglia BT, 95° Gruppo BT, 35° Stormo BT, which operated over Greece in the 1941 campaign.

Specification: Cant Z.1007bis Alcione
Type: five-crew medium bomber/torpedo-bomber
Powerplant: three 1,000-hp (746-kW) Piaggio P.XIbis RC 40 radial pistons
Performance: max speed 280 mph (450 km/h) at 13,780 ft (4200 m); initial climb rate 1,542 ft (470 m) per minute; ceiling 26,575 ft (8100 m); range 800 miles (1280 km)
Weights: empty 19,005 lb (8620 kg); max take-off 30,029 lb (13621 kg)
Dimensions: span 81 ft 4½ in (24.80 m); length 60 ft 2½ in (18.35 m); height 17 ft 1½ in (5.22 m); wing area 75.35 sq ft (70.00 m²)
Armament: two beam 7.7-mm (0.303-in) Breda SAFAT guns, dorsal & ventral 12.7-mm (0.5-in) guns; bombs 4,409 lb (2000 kg) internally, 2,205 lb (1000 kg) underwing, or two 1,000-lb (454-kg) torpedoes

Consolidated B-24 Liberator

On account of its very long range, the Liberator was ideal as a maritime patrol aircraft and served with both the US Navy and RAF Coastal Command, based in Britain. This PB4Y-1 of US Navy squadron VPB-110 was based in the UK during the winter of 1944-45.

Produced in larger numbers than any other American aircraft during the war (and any other four-engined aircraft in history), the **B-24** did not enter the design stage until 1939; the prototype **XB-24** was flown on 29 December. Minor development batches followed in 1940 before the first major production version, the **B-24D**, appeared late in 1941. The concentration of B-24s primarily in the Pacific theatre (where its long range was used to good effect) resulted in most of the 2,738 B-24Ds being deployed against Japan, but the 8th and 9th Air Forces in Europe and North Africa also received the aircraft, one of their outstanding raids being the attack on the Ploesti oil refineries on 1 August 1943. A total of 791 **B-24E**s with changed propellers was produced before production switched to the **B-24G** (430 built). This version introduced a two-gun nose turret to counter German head-on fighter attacks, and was followed by 3,100 **B-24H**s. Major production version was the **B-24J**, of which 6,678 were built, incorporating a Motor Products nose turret, new-type autopilot and bomb sight. The **B-24L** (1,667 built) featured two manually-operated guns in a Consolidated turret, and the

B-24M (2,593 built) introduced a Motor Products two-gun tail turret. This huge effort (producing a total of 18,313 aircraft in 5½ years) involved Consolidated, Douglas, Ford and North American plants, the total including many aircraft for the RAF (in which Liberators served with 42 squadrons) and US Navy (with whom Liberators served under the designation **PB4Y**), and also the 25-passenger **C-87** version, of which 282 were produced.

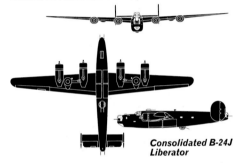

Consolidated B-24J Liberator

Specification:
Consolidated B-24J Liberator
Type: eight/10-crew daylight medium/heavy bomber
Powerplant: four 1,200-hp (895-kW) Pratt & Whitney R-1830-65 radial pistons
Performance: max speed 290 mph (467 km/h) at 25,000 ft (620 m); climb to 20,000 ft (6095 m) in 25 minutes; ceiling 28,000 ft (8535 m); range 2,000 miles (3219 km)
Weights: empty 36,500 lb (16556 kg); max take-off 65,000 lb (29484 kg)
Dimensions: span 110 ft 0 in (33.53 m); length 67 ft 2 in (20.47 m); height 18 ft 0 in (5.49 m); wing area 1,048.0 sq ft (97.36 m²)
Armament: two-gun turrets in nose, tail, upper and under fuselage, single flexible guns in waist positions to total 10 0.5-in (12.7-mm) guns; bomb load 8,800 lb (3992 kg)

The USAAF employed a unique expedient to assist in assembling its large formations of bombers, using a brightly painted aircraft (in this case covered with polka dots) on which component leaders would formate. Once the whole formation had caught up, the 'assembly ship' returned to base.

Consolidated PBY Catalina

Catalinas flew with a total of 18 squadrons of the RAF, almost all with Coastal Command. This Catalina Mk IV of No. 210 Sqn, with ASV Mk II radar, was based at Sullom Voe in the Shetlands for patrol duties over the Denmark Straits in 1944-45.

The prototype of the **Catalina** flying-boat was the **XP3Y-1** that first flew on 28 March 1935. Giving the type a substantial bomb-carrying capability brought it into the patrol bomber category so that production aircraft were termed **PBY-1s**, and these first equipped USN squadron VP-11F in October 1936. Similar **PBY-2s** and **PBY-3s** followed into service in 1937-38. The **PBY-4**, introduced in 1938, featured 1,050-hp (783-kW) Pratt & Whitney R-1830-72 radials and large transparent blister fairings over the beam gunners' positions (previously covered by sliding hatches). By the end of 1941, 16 US Navy squadrons were flying the **PBY-5** with -92 engines and modified fin shape; in addition, five squadrons were still equipped with earlier versions. At the time of Pearl Harbor, the first examples of the **PBY-5A** amphibian were being delivered. Substantial numbers of PBY-4s and PBY-5s had been ordered by the UK, and within three years these totalled 685, many delivered to the air forces of Canada, Australia and New Zealand as well as RAF Coastal Command. A version with heightened fin and rudder, and search radar in a fairing above the cockpit, was the **PBY-6A**, 112 being delivered

to the US Navy, 48 to Russia and 75 to the USAAF (as the **OA-10B**). Production was undertaken in Canada by Canadian Vickers and Boeing, the version which joined the RCAF being called the **Canso**; the Naval Aircraft Factory at Philadelphia produced the **PBN-1 Nomad** with improvements to hull and tip floats. Total production of all versions of the PBY was 3,290 in the US and Canada, plus an unknown quantity built in Russia as the **GST**.

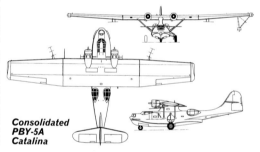

Consolidated PBY-5A Catalina

Capable of remaining on patrol for 24 hours at a time, the graceful PBY-5 Catalina equipped 16 US Navy patrol squadrons when America entered the war in 1941. The aircraft is here seen on patrol over the Aleutians in the North Pacific and is carrying early ASV radar.

**Specification:
Consolidated PBY-2 Catalina**
Type: seven/nine-crew patrol bomber flying-boat
Powerplant: two 900-hp (671.4-kW) Pratt & Whitney R-1830-64 radials
Performance: max speed 178 mph (286 km/h) at 8,000 ft (2438 m); climb rate 830 ft (253 m) per minute; service ceiling 20,800 ft (6340 m); range 2,110 miles (3396 km)
Weights: empty 14,668 lb (6653 kg); gross 28,400 lb (12882 kg)
Dimensions: span 104 ft 0 in (31.69 m); length 65 ft 10 in (20.07 m); height 18 ft 6 in (5.64 m); wing area 1,400 sq ft (130 m²)
Armament: two 0.3-in (7.62-mm) and two 0.50-in (12.7-mm) machine-guns; four 1,000-lb (454-kg) bombs

Curtiss P-40 Warhawk

This P-40L of the 325th Fighter Group based in Tunisia flew escort duties for medium bombers of the USAAF's 47th Bomb Wing in 1943. The P-40 was generally inferior to other contemporary British and American fighters.

America's most important fighter at the time of Pearl Harbor, the **P-40** gave valuable service throughout the war. It had first flown as the **X17Y** (the **P-36** with Pratt & Whitney R-1830 radial) and been re-engined as the **XP-40** with a supercharged Allison V-1710 inline engine in October 1938. Large orders followed, most P-40As going to the RAF (**Tomahawk Mk I**). The **P-40B** (**Tomahawk Mk IA** in the RAF) followed with cockpit armour and an armament of two 0.5-in (12.7-mm) and four 0.3-in (7.62-mm) guns. The **P-40C** (**Tomahawk Mk IIB**) featured self-sealing fuel tanks. The **P-40D** introduced a shortened nose with radiator moved forward and deepened, this marked change in appearance being identified by a change of name to **Kittyhawk** in the RAF (all P-40s in American service being termed **Warhawks**); the P-40D corresponded with the **Kittyhawk Mk I**. The first major USAAF version was the **P-40E** (**Kittyhawk Mk IA**) with six 0.5-in (12.7-mm) wing guns, 2,320 of which were built. A Packard-built Rolls-Royce Merlin powered the **P-40F** (**Kittyhawk Mk II**). The most-produced version was the **P-40N** (**Kittyhawk Mk IV**) (5,219 built), which reverted to the Allison V-1710 engine and featured shackles for up to 1,500 lb (680 kg) of bombs. The majority of USAAF P-40s served in the Pacific, although many served in the Mediterranean theatre alongside the RAF's Tomahawks and Kittyhawks. Total USAAF production was 12,014, of which 1,182 Tomahawks and 3,342 Kittyhawks were built on British contracts.

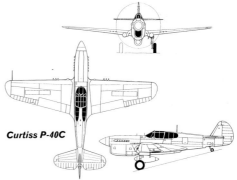

Curtiss P-40C

Specification: Curtiss P-40N-20 Warhawk (Kittyhawk Mk V)

Type: single-seat fighter/fighter-bomber
Powerplant: one 1,360-hp (1015-kW) Allison V-1710-81 inline piston
Performance: max speed 378 mph (609 km/h) at 10,500 ft (3200 m); climb to 15,000 ft (4570 m) in 6.7 minutes; service ceiling 38,000 ft (11580 m); range 240 miles (386 km)
Weights: empty 6,000 lb (2722 kg); max take-off 11,400 lb (5171 kg)
Dimensions: span 37 ft 4 in (11.38 m); length 33 ft 4 in (10.16 m); height 12 ft 4 in (3.76 m); wing area 236.0 sq ft (21.92 m²)
Armament: six 0.5-in (12.7-mm) machine-guns in wings; bomb load up to three 500-lb (227-kg) bombs

Although P-40Bs and P-40Cs were in combat with the Japanese from the start of the Pacific war, the P-40E (shown here) was the first version to serve with the USAAF in Europe and the Middle East in 1942.

Curtiss SB2C Helldiver

So important was the SB2C considered to be that the entire production (other than 26 Canadian-built aircraft destined for the Royal Air Force) was retained for use by the US Navy and Marine Corps.

Last of a long line of Curtiss aircraft to carry the name **Helldiver** (the earlier aircraft being inter-war biplanes), the **SB2C** was first flown as the **XSB2C-1** on 18 December 1940. Production **SB2C-1**s featured an enlarged fin and rudder assembly, increased fuel capacity and four 0.5-in (12.7-mm) guns in the wings. The **SB2C-1C** carried an armament of two 20-mm guns in the wings. The **SB2C-3** appeared in 1944 with a more powerful engine, and the **SB2C-4** had provision to carry eight 5-in (127-mm) rockets or 1,000 lb (454 kg) of bombs under the wings (in addition to the 1,000-lb/454-kg internal bomb load). The **SB2C-4E** featured radar in a small pod under the wing, and the **SB2C-5** carried increased fuel. Production amounted to 7,199 of all aircraft, including 300 by Fairchild in Canada, 984 by the Canadian Car and Foundry Co., and 900 produced for the USAAF as the **A-25A** (most of which were taken over by the US Marine Corps and redesignated **SB2C-1A**). Some 450 Canadian CCF-built Helldivers were ordered for the Royal Navy; in the event, only 26 **SBW-1B** aircraft were delivered to the UK by 1944, and they did not see service.

Helldivers first went into action on 11 November 1943 with a raid by VB-17 on Rabaul. During 1944 the type gradually replaced the Douglas SBD Dauntless, with the aircraft seeing constant action against the Japanese.

Curtiss SB2C Helldiver

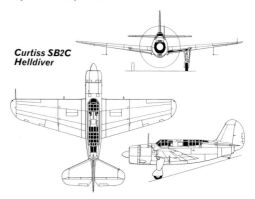

The Curtiss Helldiver was flown in large numbers by the US Navy and Marine Corps in the last two years of the Pacific war. The SB2C was a fairly large aeroplane by the standards of World War II carrier aircraft, spanning almost 50 ft (15 m).

Specification: Curtiss SB2C-4 Helldiver
Type: two-seat scout-bomber
Powerplant: one 1,900-hp (1417-kW) Wright R-2600-20 radial piston
Performance: max speed 295 mph (476 km/h) at 16,700 ft (5090 m); initial climb rate 1,800 ft (549 m) per minute; service ceiling 29,100 ft (8870 m); range 1,165 miles (1875 km)
Weights: empty 10,547 lb (4784 kg); max take-off 16,616 lb (7537 kg)
Dimensions: span 49 ft 9 in (15.16 m); length 36 ft 8 in (11.17 m); height 13 ft 2 in (4.01 m); wing area 422.0 sq ft (39.20 m²)
Armament: two fixed forward-firing 20-mm guns in wings, two 0.3-in (7.62-mm) flexible guns in rear cockpit; bomb load 1,000 lb (454 kg) under wings and 1,000 lb (454 kg) internally

de Havilland Mosquito

One of the first squadrons to receive the Mosquito Mk IV was No. 139 Sqn at Horsham St Faith in September 1942, one of whose aircraft is shown here. Two No. 139 Sqn Mosquitoes carried out a historic daylight raid on Berlin in January 1943.

Conceived in 1938 as a private venture and employing a primarily wooden structure to off-set dependence on strategic materials, the twin Merlin-powered **de Havilland Mosquito** first flew on 25 November 1940. It entered RAF service in a photo-reconnaissance role (Mosquito **Mk I**) in mid-1941, then as a high-speed unarmed bomber (**B.Mk IV**) and night-fighter with four 20-mm plus four 0.303-in (7.7-mm) guns (**NF.Mk II**), both in May 1942. The **T.Mk III** was a trainer and the **FB.Mk VI** a fighter-bomber capable of carrying two 500-lb (227-kg) bombs in the rear of the bomb bay. In 1944 the **B.Mk IX** joined Bomber Command's night offensive, carrying a single 4,000-lb (1814-kg) bomb in an enlarged bomb bay, a weapon it later carried to Berlin. B.Mk IXs were also fitted with Oboe, the pathfinding radar device. Developed from the Mk IX was the Mosquito **B.Mk XVI**, also a 4,000-lb (1814-kg) bomb carrier but with pres-surised cabin and wing drop tank provision. Photo-reconnaissance versions included the **PR.Mks VIII** and **XVI** high-altitude aircraft, the very long-range **PR.Mk XVI** high-altitude aircraft, and the very long-range **PR.Mk 34**, intended for the Far East. As a

night-fighter, the Mk II was followed by the **NF.Mks XII** and **XIII** with airborne radar (Mk VIII), the **NF.Mk XVII** with American Mk X radar, and the high-altitude **NF.Mk 30**. The anti-shipping **FB.Mk XVIII** carried a 57-mm Molins gun in the nose. Total Mosquito production was 7,781, including air-craft built in Canada and Australia.

de Havilland
Mosquito
B.Mk XVI

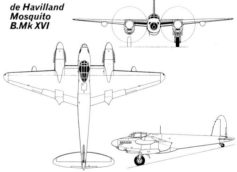

Specification:
de Havilland Mosquito
PR.Mk 34
Type: two-seat photo-reconnaissance aircraft
Powerplant: two 1,710-hp (1276-kW) Rolls-Royce Merlin 76 or 113 inline pistons
Performance: max speed 425 mph (684 km/h) at 30,500 ft (9295 m); climb to 15,000 ft (4570 m) in 72 minutes; service ceiling 36,000 ft (10970 m); range 3,500 miles (5633 km)
Weights: empty 16,631 lb (7544 kg); max take-off 25,500 lb (11567 kg)
Dimensions: span 54 ft 2 in (16.51 m); length 41 ft 6 in (12.65 m); height 15 ft 3 in (4.65 m); wing area 454.0 sq ft (42.18 m²)
Armament: none

The superb Mosquito epitomised the fast light bomber whose sole protection lay in its speed; until the advent of jet aircraft, it was virtually beyond the reach of any defending fighter. Built almost entirely of wood, the aircraft was powered by two Rolls-Royce Merlins.

Dewoitine D.520

If the French aircraft industry had met its delivery schedules in 1939 and 1940, fortunes would have been different for the French air force. This D.520 is from the escadrille de chasse, SNCASE factory at Toulouse, June 1940.

Best French fighter at the time of the German attack of May 1940 was the **Dewoitine D.520**, probably equivalent to the RAF's Hurricane Mk I. Only 36 had been delivered to a single *groupe de chasse* when the blow fell. Although the need for a fighter to replace the D.510 had been acknowledged as long ago as 1934, the D.520's design was not started until November 1936; the prototype was flown by Marcel Doret on 2 October 1938. Such delays were symptoms of the lethargy and procrastination that pervaded the French aircraft industry immediately before the war. It was not until 2 November 1939 that the first production D.520 was flown. First to receive the new fighter was GC 1/3, and this *groupe* first met the Luftwaffe on 13 May, when it shot down three Hs 126s and an He 111 without loss. Some 43 other aircraft were quickly delivered to GC II/3, GC II/7, GC III/3 and GC III/6 and, as new aircraft were completed, Aéronavale *escadrilles* AC 1, 2, 3 and 4 were equipped with an additional 52 before the armistice was signed. As production of the D.520 continued in the Vichy (unoccupied) zone a number of French pilots escaped to the UK, and in due course a total of 235 D.520s served with Vichy forces in France and 202 in Africa. The highest-scoring French fighter pilot was Adjutant Pierre Le Gloan of GC III/6, who destroyed 18 enemy aircraft (out of his eventual total of 22) while flying D.520s.

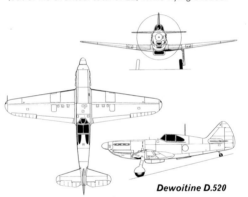

Dewoitine D.520

Following the Torch landings in North Africa in late 1942, the Germans seized the Vichy air force's 1,876 aircraft, which included 246 D.520s. Total production of the type was 775.

Specification:
Dewoitine D.520S (first 558 aircraft)
Type: single-seat fighter
Powerplant: one 930-hp (694-kW) Hispano-Suiza 12Y45 inline piston
Performance: max speed 332 mph (535 km/h) at 18,045 ft (5500 m); climb to 13,125 ft (4000 m) in 5.82 minutes; service ceiling 33,630 ft (10250 m); normal range 553 miles (890 km)
Weights: empty 4,685 lb (2125 kg); normal loaded 5,897 lb (2675 kg)
Dimensions: span 33 ft 5½ in (10.20 m); length 28 ft 8¾ in (8.76 m); height 8 ft 5¼ in (2.57 m); wing area 171.7 sq ft (15.95 m²)
Armament: one 20-mm HS404 hub-firing cannon and four 7.5-mm (0.295-in) MAC 1934 M39 machine-guns in wings

Dornier Do 17

This Dornier Do 17Z-2 belonged to 1. Staffel, Kampfgeschwader 2 'Holzhammer' based at Tatoi, Greece in May 1941. The emblem of 1./KG 2 – an eagle carrying a bomb – is painted underneath the cockpit.

The twin-engined **Dornier Do 17** first appeared in prototype form with single fin and rudder, but the exceptionally slim fuselage resulted in the aircraft being abandoned on account of cramped accommodation. The prototypes were re-evaluated as high-speed bombers and, with twin fins and rudders, the Do 17 was ordered into production as the **Do 17E** and **Do 17F**, bomber and reconnaissance versions, respectively. In 1936, both versions saw considerable service in the Spanish Civil War from 1937. Other pre-war versions were the **Do 17M** bomber and the **Do 17P** reconnaissance aircraft, these being standard service aircraft with the Luftwaffe during 1939-40. The former had 900-hp (671-kW) Bramo radials and the latter 865-hp (645-kW) BMW 132N radials. The most important version was the **Do 17Z**, which featured a deepened and glazed nose. Some idea of the importance attached to this version by the Luftwaffe may be gained by the 352 aircraft on operational charge at the end of 1939. These four-seat bombers were produced in a number of versions: the **Do 17Z-1** with four 7.92-mm (0.31-in) guns and a bomb load of 1,102 lb (500 kg); the **Do 17Z-2** with 1,000-hp

(746-kW) Bramo engines and up to eight 7.92-mm (0.31-in) guns and a bomb load of 2,205 lb (1000 kg); the **Do 17Z-3**, a photo-reconnaissance aircraft; the **Do 17Z-4**, a dual-control trainer; and the **Do 17Z-6** and **Do 17Z-10 Kauz** (Screech Owl) night-fighters, the last, produced in 1940, with two 20-mm and four 7.92-mm (0.31-in) guns.

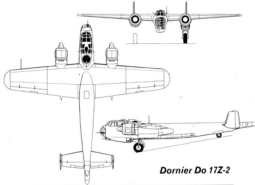

Dornier Do 17Z-2

Specification: Dornier Do 17Z-2
Type: four-crew medium bomber
Powerplant: two 1,000-hp (746-kW) Bramo 323P radial pistons
Performance: max speed 255 mph (410 km/h) at 13,125 ft (4000 m); service ceiling 26,900 ft (8200 m); max range 845 miles (1360 km)
Weights: empty 11,486 lb (5210 kg); max take-off 18,937 lb (8590 kg)
Dimensions: span 59 ft 0⅝ (18.00 m); length 52 ft 9¾ in (16.10 m); height 14 ft 11¼ in (4.55 m); wing area 592.01 sq ft (55.00 m²)
Armament: bomb load up to 2,205 lb (1000 kg); variable defensive armament of up to eight 7.92-mm (0.31-in) MG 15 flexible guns disposed around crew cabin

The Do 17 was the least effective of the Do 17/Ju 88/He 111 trio used during the early years, being slower and carrying a lighter bomb load than the other two. The type had been designed to meet a commercial requirement for a high-speed mailplane issued in 1933.

Dornier Do 18

A small number of Do 18s were used for training in coastal reconnaissance and air-sea rescue work. This Do 18D was flown by the FFS(See), Flugzeugfuhrerschule, or maritime pilot school, in the summer of 1939.

The first **Dornier Do 18V1** was flown on 15 March 1935 and the first military variant, the **Do 18D**, was operational with the Luftwaffe in September 1938. Powered by two tandem-aligned Jumo 205C engines and with a four-man crew, the **Do 18D-1** and **Do 18D-2** carried single flexible 7.92-mm (0.31-in) machine-guns in bow and midships positions. By the outbreak of war the **Do 18G**, with 880-hp (656-kW) Jumo 205D engines, a 13-mm (0.51-in) bow gun and a turret-mounted 20-mm cannon amidships, had entered production and joined earlier versions with the *Kustenfliegergruppen* (coastal reconnaissance groups) for duties over the North Sea and Baltic. After about 100 aircraft (including some 70 Do 18Gs) had been completed, production was halted, but the flying-boats continued in service until 1942. The **Do 18H** trainer was produced by converting some Do 18Gs to include dual controls, and the **Do 18N** air-sea rescue aircraft were also modified from Do 18Gs to carry ambulance equipment, working with the *Seenotstaffeln* (air sea rescue squadrons) in France, Denmark, the Netherlands and Norway. It was, incidentally, a coastal reconnaissance Do 18

of 2./KuFlGr 106 that was the first German aircraft to fall victim to British air action in the war when it was shot down by Blackburn Skuas from HMS *Ark Royal* over the North Sea on 26 September 1939.

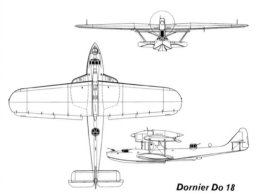

Dornier Do 18

The Do 18D (Do 18G shown here) was the first version of this flying-boat to serve with the Luftwaffe's **Kustenfliegergruppen** *(coastal reconnaissance groups). The type originated as a commercial aircraft ordered by the airline Deutsche Lufthansa in 1934 to replace the highly successful but ageing Wal (Whale).*

Specification: Dornier Do 18G-1
Type: four-crew coastal reconnaissance flying-boat
Powerplant: two 880-hp (656-kW) Junkers Jumo 205D tandem inline pistons
Performance: max speed 162 mph (260 km/h) at sea level; climb to 3,280 ft (1000 m) in 7.9 minutes; service ceiling 13,780 ft (4200 m); range 2,174 miles (3500 km)
Weights: empty 12,900 lb (5850 kg); max take-off 22,046 lb (10000 kg)
Dimensions: span 77 ft 9 in (23.70 m); length 63 ft 2 in (19.25 m); height 17 ft 5½ in (5.32 m); wing area 1,049 sq ft (97.5 m²)
Armament: one 13-mm (0.51-in) MG 131 gun in bow flexible mounting and one 20-mm MG 151 gun in midships turret; 220 lb (100 kg) of bombs

Dornier Do 217

The Dornier Do 217E was widely used in the anti-shipping role over the Atlantic and North Sea from 1941 to 1943. This Do 217E-2 (with ship tally on the fin) served with 6. Staffel, Kampfgeschwader 40, at Bordeaux-Merignac late in 1942.

Just as the Dornier Do 17 was entering service, the manufacturers proposed a larger and faster version; this was the **Do 217**, whose **Do 217V1** prototype with two 1,075-hp (802-kW) Daimler-Benz DB 601A inline engines first flew in August 1938. Directional stability problems led to larger tail surfaces on pre-production **Do 217A-0** reconnaissance aircraft, which joined the Luftwaffe in 1940 and carried out clandestine flights over Soviet territory. First production version was the **Do 217E-1** bomber with two 1,550-hp (1156-kW) BMW 801MA radials, a crew of four or five, and a bomb load of 4,409 lb (2000 kg); it first joined II./KG 40 in France in March 1941. Following versions included the **Do 217E-2** with dorsal turret added and 13-mm (0.51-in) gun in addition to the normal armament of one 13-mm (0.51-in), one 15-mm (0.59-in) and up to five 7.92-mm (0.31-in) guns; the **Do 217E-3** with additional armour; and the Do **217E-5**, adapted to carry two Henschel Hs 293 anti-shipping missiles. The **Do 217J** night-fighter, with FuG 202 radar, two 20-mm and four 7.92-mm (0.31-in) guns in the nose, joined the Luftwaffe in 1942. The **Do 217K** bomber was powered by 1,700-hp (1268-kW)

BMW 801D engines and was produced in versions adapted to carry Hs 293 or Fritz X missiles. Produced simultaneously was the **Do 217M** with 1,750-hp (1306-kW) DB 603As, with sub-variants similar to those of the Do 217K. Final main variant was the **Do 217N** night-fighter with DB 603As and four 20-mm and four 7.92-mm (0.31-in) guns, plus two 20-mm upward-firing guns (all in the nose).

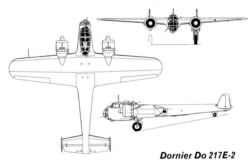

Dornier Do 217E-2

Specification: Dornier Do 217M-1
Type: four-crew heavy bomber
Powerplant: two 1,750-hp (1306-kW) Daimler-Benz DB 603A inline pistons
Performance: max speed 348 mph (560 km/h) at 18,700 ft (5700 km); initial climb rate 688 ft (210 m) per minute; service ceiling 31,170 ft (9500 m); normal range 1,335 miles (2150 km)
Weights: empty 19,845 lb (9000 kg); max take-off 36,817 lb (16700 kg)
Dimensions: span 62 ft 4 in (19.00 m); length 58 ft 4½ in (17.79 m); height 16 ft 6 in (5.03 m); wing area 613.54 sq ft (57.00 m²)
Armament: two 13-mm (0.51-in) and up to six 7.92-mm (0.31-in) guns; 8,818 lb (4000 kg) of bombs, 5,511 lb (2500 kg) carried internally

The Do 217 was a larger and faster version of the Do 17, and an eventual total of 1,730 was built. The type was regarded as an efficient and reliable bomber and night-fighter, on which the Luftwaffe came to rely heavily during the last three years of the war.

Douglas A-20/DB-7 Boston/Havoc

Known as the Havoc when serving as a night-fighter in the RAF, the aircraft was also widely used in 1941 as an 'intruder bomber'. The aircraft depicted here belonged to No. 23 Sqn based at Ford; their job was later taken over by Beaufighters and Mosquitoes.

The Douglas Model 7A evolved into the **DB-7** for foreign air forces in 1937, and a prototype was flown on 17 August 1939. Orders were placed principally by the French government but, with the fall of France in 1940, most of the aircraft were taken over by the RAF where they were modified as night-fighters with eight 0.303-in (7.7-mm) guns in the nose as the **Havoc Mk I** (and with 12 guns as the **Mk II**). The USAAF placed initial contracts for 206 **A-20**s and **A-20A**s, the former with tur-bocharged Wright R-2600 7 radials being the USAAF's fastest **Havoc**. Minor alterations to the nose shape identified the **A-20B** (999 produced), while **DB-7B**s and **-7C**s were repossessed from the British and Dutch, respectively. The **A-20C** was an attempt to standardise British and American requirements in a single version but, with gross weight advancing to 25,600 lb (11612 kg), the maximum speed fell to 342 mph (550 km/h). The A-20C was the first USAAF version to see combat, the 15th Bomb Squadron arriving in the UK in May 1942 (flying its first operations in **Boston Mk IIIC**s of the RAF's No. 226 Squadron on 4 July 1942). The most produced version was the **A-20G** (2,850

completed); early aircraft were armed with four 20-mm and two 0.5-in (12.7-mm) nose guns, but later versions had the cannon deleted in favour of four more 0.5-in (12.7-mm) guns, and external racks doubled the bomb load to 4,000 lb (1814 kg). The A-20G was followed by 412 **A-20H**s, with more powerful engines. Total production of all A-20s was 7,385, including 3,125 for the Soviet Union.

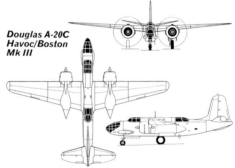

Douglas A-20C Havoc/Boston Mk III

The Douglas A-20/DB-7 was ordered by a number of air forces, including those of France, the United Kingdom, the USSR and the United States (one of whose A-20Gs is seen here). A versatile and reliable design, the DB-7 first flew on 17 August 1939.

Specification: Douglas A-20G Havoc
Type: three-crew light attack bomber
Powerplant: two 1,600-hp (1194-kW) Wright R-2600-23 radial pistons
Performance: max speed 339 mph (546 km/h) at 12,400 ft (3780 m); climb to 10,000 ft (3050 m) in 7.1 minutes; service ceiling 25,800 ft (7865 m); range 1,090 miles (1754 km)
Weights: empty 15,984 lb (7250 kg); max take-off 27,200 lb (12338 kg)
Dimensions: span 61 ft 4 in (18.69 m); length 48 ft 0 in (14.63 m); height 17 ft 7 in (5.36 m); wing area 464.0 sq ft (43.11 m²)
Armament: six 0.5-in (12.7-mm) machine-guns in nose and two 0.5-in (12.7-mm) machine-guns in dorsal turret; bomb load up to 2,600 lb (1179 kg)

Douglas A-26 Invader

Employing the remotely-controlled gun turrets developed in America during the war, the A-26B was armed with a total of 10 0.5-in (12.7-mm) machine-guns, including a battery of six in the nose, plus a bomb load of 4,000 lb (1814 kg).

Designed in 1940 to replace the A-20 Havoc – and incorporating the fruits of early wartime experience – the **Douglas A-26** was the last important American aircraft in the category of 'attack' bomber. The first of three prototypes, the **XA-26**, was flown on 10 July 1942 as a bomber with bombardier's glazed nose station; the second (the **XA-26A**) was a night-fighter prototype with four 20-mm guns under the fuselage and four 0.5-in (12.7-mm) guns in a remotely-controlled dorsal turret; and the third (**XA 26B**) was armed with a 75-mm cannon in the nose. The heavily armoured **A-26B** was selected for production, capable of carrying a maximum bomb load of 6,000 lb (2722 kg) plus eight 0.5-in (12.7-mm) rocket projectiles. A total of 1,355 A-26Bs was built, deliveries to the USAAF starting in 1944 with 2,000-hp (1492-kW) Pratt & Whitney R-2800 engines; with their speed of 355 mph (572 km/h) they were among the fastest of all American wartime bombers. The only other version produced during the war was the **A-26C**, in which all but two of the six nose 0.5-in (12.7-mm) guns were deleted, being replaced by a transparent bombardier's station; a total of 1,091 A-26Cs was produced, most of which were delivered to the Pacific theatre, and 88 A-26Cs were supplied to the US Navy. Over 5,250 A-26s were cancelled at the end of the war, although the aircraft (later redesignated the **B-26** when the Martin Marauder had disappeared from service) was widely used by the post-war USAF, particularly in the Korean War.

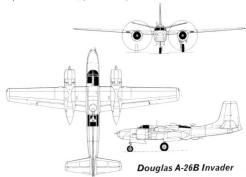

Douglas A-26B Invader

Specification: Douglas A-26B-1 Invader
Type: three-crew light attack bomber
Powerplant: two 2,000-hp (1492-kW) Pratt & Whitney R-2800-79 radial pistons
Performance: max speed 355 mph (572 km/h) at 16,000 ft (4875 m); climb to 10,000 ft (3050 m) in 8.1 minutes; service ceiling 22,100 ft (6735 m); range 1,400 miles (2253 km)
Weights: empty 22,370 lb (10147 kg); max take-off 35,000 lb (15880 kg)
Dimensions: span 70 ft 0 in (21.35 m); length 50 ft 9 in (15.47 m); height 18 ft 6 in (5.64 m); wing area 540.0 sq ft (50.17 m²)
Armament: six 0.5-in (12.7-mm) guns in nose, two 0.5-in (12.7-mm) guns each in dorsal and ventral turrets; 6,000 lb (2722 kg) of bombs, eight 5-in (127-mm) rockets

These formations of Douglas A-26s, attached to the 386th Bomb Group, are seen en route to bomb enemy installations somewhere in Germany on 20 April 1945. The Invader only reached operational units during the final months of hostilities, joining the 9th Air Force in Europe in November 1944.

Douglas SBD Dauntless

After the Allied landings of November 1942 in North Africa, the French naval air service was given 32 Dauntless aircraft. In 1944, after a period in training, these were flown to Cognac in southern France to support French ground forces.

Developed directly from the Northrop BT-1 (the Northrop Corporation became a division of Douglas), the prototype of the **SBD Dauntless** two-seat carrierborne dive-bomber was in fact a much modified production BT-1. Production orders for 57 **SBD-1**s and 87 **SBD-2**s were placed in April 1939, the former being delivered to US Marine Corps bombing and scout-bombing squadrons, and the latter to US Navy scout and bombing squadrons. The **SBD-3**, with two additional 0.5-in (12.7-mm) guns in the nose, self-sealing tanks and R-1829-52 engine, appeared in March 1941, and by the time of Pearl Harbor in December that year 584 SBD-3s had been delivered. Some 780 **SBD-4**s (with 24-volt system but otherwise similar to the SBD-3 and produced at El Segundo, California) were built in 1942; photo-reconnaissance modifications – the **SBD-1P**, **SBD-2P** and **SBD-3P** – were also produced during 1941-42. A new Douglas plant at Tulsa, Oklahoma, produced 2,409 **SBD-5**s with 1,200-hp (895-kW) R-1820-60 engines, following these with 451 **SBD-6**s with -66 engines. The USAAF took delivery of 168 **SBD-3A**, 170 **SBD-4A** and 615 **SBD-5A** aircraft as the **A-24**, **A-24A** and **A-24B**, respectively, bringing the total Douglas production to 5,321 SBDs. They were unquestionably one of the USA's most important weapons in the Pacific war, and sank a greater tonnage of Japanese shipping than any other aircraft, as well as playing a key part in the great battles of Midway, the Coral Sea and the Solomons.

Douglas SBD Dauntless

A formation of Douglas SBD Dauntless scout bombers. This aircraft bore the brunt of carrierborne bombing duties in the Pacific between 1942 and 1944, serving aboard such famous American carriers as the USS Lexington, Saratoga, Yorktown and Enterprise.

Specification: Douglas SBD-5 Dauntless
Type: two-crew carrier-based scout/dive-bomber
Powerplant: one 1,200-hp (895-kW) Wright R-1820-60 radial piston
Performance: max speed 245 mph (394 km/h) at 15,800 ft (4815 m); initial climb rate 1,190 ft (363 m) per minute; ceiling 24,300 ft (7405 m); range 1,100 miles (1770 km)
Weights: empty 6,675 lb (3028 kg); max take-off 10,855 lb (4924 kg)
Dimensions: span 41 ft 6¼ in (12.65 m); length 33 ft 0⅛ in (10.06 m); height 12 ft 11 in (3.94 m); wing area 325.0 sq ft (30.19 m²)
Armament: two fixed forward-firing 0.5-in (12.7-mm) guns, two flexible 0.3-in (7.62-mm) guns in rear cockpit; one 1,600-lb (726-kg) bomb under fuselage, two 325-lb (147 kg) bombs under wings

Douglas C-47 Skytrain

This Dakota Mk III is from the RAF's No. 24 Sqn. No. 24 for many years was the RAF's principal communications squadron and flew Dakotas on frequent services between the various war fronts.

The **Douglas C-47** evolved from the DC-3 airliner which introduced new levels of speed and comfort to air travel in the late 1930s. First flown as a commercial aircraft on 15 December 1935, the C-47 was not ordered by the USAAC until 1940; the airline interior gave way to bucket seats along the cabin sides, and Pratt & Whitney R-1830 radials replaced the DC-3's Wright Cyclones. Some 953 C-47s were built before production switched to the **C-47A** with a 24-volt in place of 12-volt electrical system; a total of 4,931 C-47s was built. High-altitude superchargers and R-1830-90 engines were introduced in 3,241 **C-47B**s (including 133 **TC-47B** trainers) intended for use in South East Asia. Many other variations were produced under separate designations, of which the **C-53 Sky-trooper** was the most important, being in effect an airline-standard aircraft for military purposes. Wartime military production of the C-47 reached 10,048, plus an estimated 2,700 produced in the Soviet Union as the **Lisunov Li-2**. In the USAAF the C-47 became the standard transport and glider tug in service from 1942, being flown in large numbers in every airborne forces operation during the war. Some 1,895 Dakotas served with 25 RAF squadrons, the **Dakota Mk I** corresponding to the C-47, the **Mk II** to the C-53, the **Mk III** to the C-47A and the **Mk IV** to the C-47B. As late as 1961 the USAF still had over 1,000 C-47s on its inventory, and the type was also used by the US Navy as the **R4D** in several variants.

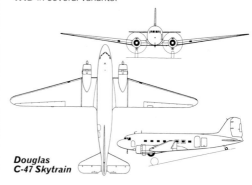

**Douglas
C-47 Skytrain**

**Specification: Douglas
C-47 Skytrain (Dakota
Mk I)**
Type: three-crew military transport
Powerplant: two 1,200-hp (895-kW) Pratt & Whitney R-1839-92 radial pistons
Performance: max speed 230 mph (370 km/h) at 8,500 ft (2590 m); climb to 10,000 ft (3050 m) in 9.6 minutes; service ceiling 24,000 ft (7315 m); range 1,600 miles (2575 km)
Weights: empty 18,200 lb (8256 kg); max take-off 26,000 lb (11805 kg)
Dimensions: span 95 ft 6 in (29.11 m); length 63 ft 9 in (19.43 m); height 17 ft 0 in (5.18 m); wing area 987.0 sq ft (91.69 m²)
Accommodation: 27 fully-armed troops or 25 paratroops, or 18-24 stretcher cases, or up to 10,000 lb (4536 kg) of freight

The C-47 (Dakota in RAF service) was probably the best known transport aeroplane of all time, whether as an airliner or military transport. Here, one of the first USAAF aircraft beats up the Douglas factory in a triumphant return from the front. Note the massed A-20s awaiting delivery in the background.

Fairey Albacore

Introducing the 'luxury' of an enclosed cabin and a Taurus engine, the Albacore was less popular with naval aircrews who generally preferred the open cockpit and rugged reliability of the older Swordfish.

The **Fairey Albacore** was in essence a cleaned-up version of the celebrated 'Stringbag' with an enclosed cabin to improve operational efficiency and a Bristol Taurus radial to provide higher performance. First flown in December 1938, the initial prototype was fitted with a wheel landing gear, while the second had twin floats. The Albacore – which was inevitably called the 'Applecore' in service – differed from the Swordfish in being used operationally only on the wheeled type of landing gear. The type entered service with the Royal Navy's Fleet Air Arm in 1940, and production amounted to 798 aircraft. The Albacore was first flown in action during attacks on Boulogne in September 1940. Most Albacores were land-based throughout their careers, but the type's brief moment of glory came when Albacores from the carrier HMS *Formidable* severely damaged the Italian battleship *Vittono Veneto* during the Battle of Cape Matapan in March 1941. After this time the Albacore was occasionally used for bombing in the Western Desert, usually at night to prevent the depredations of Axis fighters, and the type played an important part in the operations leading up to

the Battle of Alamein in October 1942. In carrier operations the Albacore was operated in the Mediterranean, and in the North Atlantic, Arctic and Indian Oceans. The type was also used with some success as a support aircraft during seaborne invasions, notably those of Sicily, Italy and northern France, the last with RCAF squadrons.

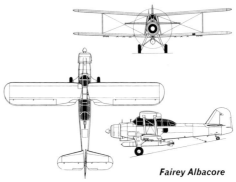

Fairey Albacore

The Fairey Albacore was almost wholly overshadowed by its stablemate, the Swordfish. Intended to supersede the latter, the Albacore nevertheless gave good service in the Mediterranean and North Africa. This example is seen dropping a practice 18-in (457-mm) torpedo.

Specification: Fairey Albacore
Type: three-crew naval torpedo-bomber
Powerplant: one 1,065-hp (794-kW) Bristol Taurus II radial piston
Performance: max speed 161 mph (259 km/h) at 7,000 ft (2135 m); climb to 6,000 ft (1830 m) in 8.0 minutes; ceiling 20,700 ft (6310 m); range 820 miles (1319 km)
Weights: empty 7,200 lb (3266 kg); max take-off 12,600 lb (5715 kg)
Dimensions: span 50 ft 0 in (15.24 m); length 39 ft 9½ in (12.13 m); height 15 ft 3 in (4.65 m); wing area 623.0 sq ft (57.88 m²)
Armament: one forward-firing 0.303-in (7.7-mm) Vickers gun, two 0.303-in (7.7-mm) Vickers 'K' guns in rear cockpit; one 18-in (45-mm) torpedo or up to 2,000 lb (907 kg) of bombs

Fairey Barracuda

The Barracuda, shown here with anti-submarine radar and underwing depth bombs, was delayed for two years by design adaptation for the Merlin engine following the discontinuation of the original powerplant.

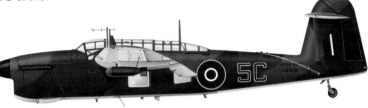

Intended to replace the Albacore (itself a replacement for the Swordfish), the **Barracuda** was designed as a high-performance monoplane to meet a 1937 requirement. The intended powerplant was the Rolls-Royce Exe, and the programme was delayed substantially when this engine was abandoned and the structure had to be revised to accommodate a Merlin engine from the same manufacturer. Thus, the Barracuda prototype did not fly until 7 December 1940, and it was immediately apparent that the performance of the heavy Barracuda would be limited by the power available: the 1,260-hp (940-kW) Merlin XXX in the Barracuda **Mk I** and the 1,640-hp (1223-kW) Merlin 32 for the Barracuda **Mks II** and **III**. At a time when production priorities were afforded mostly to the RAF, deliveries of the Barracuda to the Fleet Air Arm were slow to start, and it was January 1943 before the Barracuda Mk I began to enter service with the Fleet Air Arm. The Mk I was little more than a service-test type, only 23 being built. The two main wartime models were thus the Barracuda Mk II with ASV Mk IIN radar (1,635 built by Fairey, Blackburn, Boulton Paul and Westland) and the Barracuda Mk III torpedo-reconnaissance version with ASV Mk X radar (912 built by the parent company). The Barracuda saw limited service in home waters, its high point being a successful strike on the German battleship *Tirpitz* in April 1944, but in the Pacific campaigns of 1944 and 1945 the Barracuda was a prominent British aircraft.

Fairey Barracuda Mk II

Specification: Fairey Barracuda Mk II

Type: three-crew shipborne torpedo-/dive-bomber
Powerplant: one 1,640-hp (1223-kW) Rolls-Royce Merlin 32 inline piston
Performance: max speed 228 mph (367 km/h) at 1,750 ft (535 m); climb to 5,000 ft (1525 m) in 6.0 minutes; ceiling 16,600 ft (5060 m); range 1,150 miles (1850 km)
Weights: empty 9,350 lb (4241 kg); max take-off 14,100 lb (6396 kg)
Dimensions: span 49 ft 2 in (14.99 m); length 39 ft 9 in (12.11 m); height 15 ft 1 in (4.60 m); wing area 367.0 sq ft (34.09 m²)
Armament: two 0.303-in (7.7-mm) Vickers 'K' machine-guns in rear cockpit; one 1,620-lb (735-kg) torpedo, or four 450-lb (204-kg) depth charges, or six 250-lb (113-kg) bombs

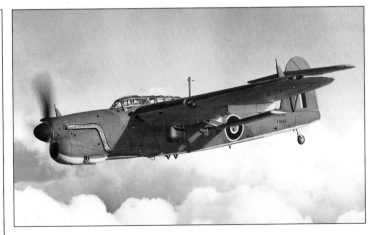

Despite its ungainly appearance, the Fairey Barracuda was intended to embody experience gained with such aircraft as the Swordfish, while at the same time benefitting from the monoplane configuration. Unfortunately, entrenched demands for naval accoutrements compromised the design from the outset.

Fairey Battle

Among the Battle squadrons which were virtually annihilated during the French campaign of May 1940 was No. 218 Sqn. The aircraft simply proved too slow in the face of accurate flak and swarming enemy fighters.

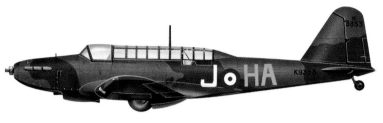

Synonymous with the tragedy that befell France in 1940, the **Fairey Battle** light bomber proved hopelessly outclassed in the presence of the modern Luftwaffe at that time, yet this aircraft had been conceived in the early 1930s as one of the key aircraft to equip the quickly expanding pre-war RAF. First flown on 10 March 1936, the Battle joined Nos 52 and 63 Squadrons in March 1937; in little over a year Battles equipped 17 day bomber squadrons. At the outbreak of war 10 Battle squadrons accompanied the Advanced Air Striking Force to France, but within a month were suffering prohibitive losses when sent on daylight raids without fighter escort. With no suitable replacement available they remained in France and constituted the RAF's day bomber force when the German Blitzkrieg opened in the west on 10 May 1940. The war's first Victoria Crosses were awarded posthumously to a Battle's crew (Flying Officer D. E. Garland and Sergeant T. Gray of No. 12 Squadron) for an attack on the Maastricht bridges on 10 May, when four out of five aircraft were shot down. In an attack at Sedan on 14 May, 40 Battles from a force of 70 were destroyed. After less than a

month the AASF had been decimated and the surviving Battles were withdrawn to the UK but, after a short period, they were withdrawn from operations and relegated to training. Many were shipped to Canada, while others undertook target-towing duties. Battles supplied to Belgium fared no better in 1940 than those of the RAF.

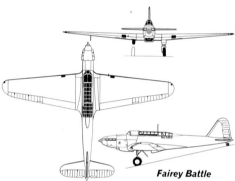

Fairey Battle

After the Fairey Battle's disastrous experiences in France during May 1940 as a light bomber, production switched to trainer versions, dual controls being provided in separate cockpits. Many Battles were also relegated to target towing.

Specification: Fairey Battle Mk I
Type: three-crew light bomber
Powerplant: one 1,030-hp (768-kW) Rolls-Royce Merlin III inline piston
Performance: max speed 241 mph (388 km/h) at 13,000 ft (3960 m); climb to 5,000 ft (1525 m) in 4.1 minutes; service ceiling 23,500 ft (7165 m); range 1,050 miles (1690 km)
Weights: empty 6,647 lb (3015 kg); max take-off 10,792 lb (4895 kg)
Dimensions: span 54 ft 0 in (16.46 m); length 45 ft 1¾ in (12.90 m); height 15 ft 6 in (4.72 m); wing area 422.0 sq ft (39 20 m²)
Armament: one fixed forward-firing 0.303-in (7.7-mm) machine-gun, one 0.303-in (7.7-mm) flexible machine-gun in rear cockpit; bomb load 1,000 lb (454 kg)

Fairey Swordfish

Pictured here is an early production Swordfish Mk I complete with 18-in (457-mm) naval torpedo. This version served in the 'torpedo-spotter reconnaissance' role during the early years of the war.

Of all aircraft regarded as anachronisms the **Fairey Swordfish** torpedo-bomber must be the supreme example for, even in the early 1930s, it appeared archaic and cumbersome. Stemming from an earlier design whose prototype had crashed, the first prototype Swordfish (the **TSR.II**) initially flew on 17 April 1934. The production Swordfish **Mk I** was prepared to Specification S 38/34 with a slightly swept-back top wing, and all-metal construction with fabric covering. By the outbreak of war in 1939 a total of 689 aircraft had been delivered or were on order, serving with both wheel and float landing gear aboard Royal Navy carriers, battleships, battle-cruisers and cruisers in the torpedo-spotter reconnaissance role. Among the memorable actions in which the word 'Stringbag' participated were the action at Taranto of 11 November 1940, when Swordfish aircraft from HMS *Illustrious* sank or crippled three Italian battleships; the crippling of the *Bismarck* in the Atlantic; and the suicidal attack on the German warships *Scharnhorst*, *Gneisenau* and *Prinz Eugen* during their famous escape up the English Channel in February 1942. Production of the Swordfish was

undertaken largely by Blackburn and included the **Mk II** with a strengthened lower wing to allow eight rocket projectiles to be mounted, the **Mk III** with ASV radar between the landing gear legs, and the **Mk IV** conversion of the Mk II with a rudimentary enclosed cabin. Production ended on 18 August 1944, with 2,396 Swordfish completed.

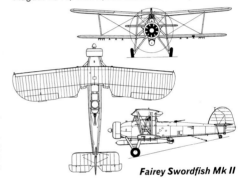

Fairey Swordfish Mk II

Specification: Fairey Swordfish Mk II

Type: three-crew torpedo/ASW aircraft

Powerplant: one 750-hp (560-kW) Bristol Pegasus XXX radial

Performance: max speed 138 mph (222 km/h) at sea level; climb rate 1,220 ft (372 m) per minute; service ceiling 19,250 ft (5865 m); range 546 miles (879 km)

Weights: empty 4,700 lb (2132 kg); max take-off 7,510 lb (3407 kg)

Dimensions: span 45 ft 6 in (12.87 m); length 35 ft 8 in (10.87 m); height 12 ft 4 in (3.76 m); wing area 607.0 sq ft (56.39 m²)

Armament: one fixed forward-firing 0.303-in (7.7-mm) gun, one flexible 0.303-in (7.7-mm) gun in rear; weapon load one 18-in (457-mm) torpedo or eight 60-lb (27.2-kg) rocket projectiles

The immortal Swordfish was outwardly an anachronism without parallel in World War II; nevertheless, its battle honours stand unsurpassed by any other British naval aircraft, headed by the famous attack on the Bismarck in the Atlantic and the raid on the Italian fleet in Taranto harbour.

Fairey Fulmar

The large and heavy Fulmar, with a second crew member, could scarcely be expected to match single-seat fighter opponents. Against enemy bombers and flying-boats it proved more successful.

The **Fairey Fulmar** tends to be overlooked in the part it played in the first three years of the war. Developed from the Fairey P.4/34 light bomber prototypes which flew in 1937, the Fulmar fleet fighter prototype was flown on 4 January 1940, with production aircraft being completed soon after. Early trials showed the aircraft to have a disappointing performance, although it was recognised as being a fairly large aeroplane with the same engine as the Hurricane single-seater. In 1942, after 127 production Fulmar **Mk Is** had been completed, the **Mk II** appeared with the 1,260-hp (940-kW) Merlin XXX, raising the top speed to 272 mph (438 km/h). Fulmar Mk Is of No. 808 Sqn of the Fleet Air Arm were listed in RAF Fighter Command's order of battle during the Battle of Britain, although they were not engaged in combat. By November 1940, Fulmars were in action from HMS *Illustrious* at the Battle of Taranto, and soon afterwards from HMS *Ark Royal* defending the vital convoys sailing to Malta. At the Battle of Cape Matapan, Fulmars from HMS *Formidable* escorted the Albacores and Swordfish which torpedoed the Italian battleship *Vittorio Veneto*. Early in 1942, as Japanese naval forces threatened Ceylon, two squadrons of Fulmars were based there as part of Colombo's air defences. When confronted for the first time by the much superior carrier-based Zero-Sen fighters, the Fulmars were utterly outclassed and almost all were shot down or damaged. A total of 450 Mk IIs was built, and some served as night-fighters.

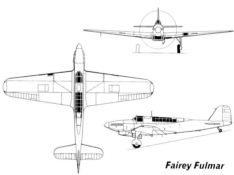

Fairey Fulmar

The Fleet Air Arm's first eight-gun carrierborne fighter, the Fulmar served with the Royal Navy throughout the first three years of the war, and despite poor performance gave good service. In the Far East, however, it proved wholly inadequate against the Japanese Zero-Sen naval fighter.

Specification: Fairey Fulmar Mk II
Type: two-seat shipborne fighter
Powerplant: one 1,260-hp (940-kW) Rolls-Royce Merlin XXX inline piston
Performance: max speed 272 mph (438 km/h) at 16,500 ft (5030 m); initial climb rate 1,320 ft (402 m) per minute; service ceiling 27,200 ft (8290 m); range 780 miles (1255 km)
Weights: empty 7,384 lb (3349 kg); max take-off 10,200 lb (4627 kg)
Dimensions: span 46 ft 4½ in (14.13 m); length 40 ft 2 in (12.24 m); height 10 ft 8 in (3.25 m); wing area 342.0 sq ft (31.77 m²)
Armament: eight 0.303-in (7.7-mm) machine-guns in wings, and a few aircraft also had a single flexible 0.303-in (7.7-mm) machine-gun in the rear cockpit

Fiat BR.20 Cicogna

This early Fiat BR.20M belonged to the 27ª Squadriglia BT, 116º Gruppo BT, 37º Stormo BT, based at Grottaglie, south Italy, late in 1940. The unit operated over the Greco-Albanian front during the invasion of Greece.

The **Fiat BR.20 Cicogna** (Stork) appeared in 1936, and a number of sporting successes and record flights by early aircraft suggested that it would become an effective addition to the Regia Aeronautica's bomber force. The first flight by the prototype on 10 February 1936 was followed by deliveries to the 13º Stormo BT in September that year, and to the 7º Stormo BT six months later. These two units took BR.20s to Spain in 1937 and, in 1938-39, 85 similar aircraft were exported to Japan for service in China. One aircraft was purchased by Venezuela in 1938. At the end of 1939 the prototype of the improved **BR.20M** was flown with cleaned-up nose and strengthened wing; the Fiat A.80 RC 41 engines remained unchanged. When Italy entered the war in June 1940, four *stormi* (the 7º, 13º, 18º and 43º) flew 148 BR.20s, roughly one-third of them the new version. Some aircraft took part in the brief campaign against France, and 80 were based in Belgium for the Italian attacks on the UK in November 1940, suffering heavy casualties. BR.20 units also suffered in night attacks on Malta, and in North Africa difficulties in operating the Fiat engines in desert condi-

tions led to considerable unserviceability – a situation which the Italian aircraft industry seemed powerless to rectify. A much improved and extensively redesigned version, the **BR.20-II** (or **BR.20bis**) had been flown in 1940 and, with 1,250-hp (933-kW) Fiat A.82 RC 32 radials, entered production in 1943. By the time of the Italian armistice only 67 BR.20s were serviceable, from 606 produced.

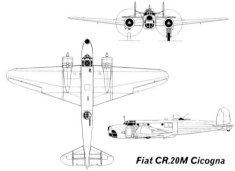

Fiat CR.20M Cicogna

Popularly referred to as the Cicogna (Stork), the Fiat BR.20 was an unimaginative design with no better than mediocre performance. It was widely used during the first two years of the war, presumably on account of its useful bomb load, but was critically short of defensive armament.

Fiat CR.42 Falco

Serving alongside the Luftwaffe at the end of the Battle of Britain, this CR.42 belonged to the 95ª Squadriglia CT, 18º Gruppo CT, 56º Stormo CT, based at Maldegen, Belgium. The CR.42s encountered a victory-flushed RAF Fighter Command and suffered heavily.

The **Fiat CR.42 Falco** (Falcon) did not first fly until 1939, and such an anachronism is difficult to understand. Employing the same Warren truss system of interplane struts as the 1933 CR.32, from which it was developed, Celestino Rosatelli's CR.42 was powered by an 840-hp (627-kW) Fiat A.74 R1C radial and had a top speed of 274 mph (441 km/h). By September 1939 the Falco equipped three *stormi* and when Italy entered the war in June 1940 there were 330 in service with four *stormi* in the Mediterranean plus two *squadriglie* in Italian East Africa. The Falco first saw combat in the brief French campaign, and later 50 aircraft accompanied the Corpo Aero Italiano to bases in Belgium for attacks on southern England at the end of the Battle of Britain, suffering heavily. In the Middle East the Falco fared better, being more of a match for the widely used Gladiator; during the Greek campaign one *gruppo* of three CR.42 *squadriglie* was committed and acquitted itself well, but when Hurricanes arrived losses mounted steadily. In East Africa, 51 crated CR.42s were received to supplement the 36 aircraft delivered to the 412ª and 413ª Squadriglie, but they were

destroyed in the air or on the ground, although they took a heavy toll of the antiquated aircraft of the RAF and SAAF. In the Western Desert, CR.42 fighters were joined by a fighter-bomber version adapted to carry two 220-lb (100-kg) bombs, which served with the 5º, 15º and 50º Stormi Assalti until November 1942. Of 1,781 CR.42s built, 64 were serviceable at the time of the Italian armistice.

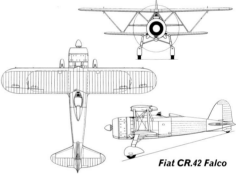

Fiat CR.42 Falco

This Fiat CR.42 Falco of the 97ª Squadriglia CT, 9º Gruppo, 4º Stormo CT, based at Benina, Libya, was captured by British forces in the Western Desert during 1940. The famous 'Cavallino Rampante' insignia has been cut from the rear fuselage by souvenir hunters.

Specification: Fiat CR.42 Falco
Type: single-seat fighter
Powerplant: one 840-hp (627-kW) Fiat A.74 R1C 38 radial piston
Performance: max speed 274 mph (441 km/h) at 19,685 ft (6000 m); climb to 19,685 ft (6000 m) in 9.0 minutes; service ceiling 33,135 ft (10100 m); range 485 miles (780 km)
Weights: empty 3,933 lb (1784 kg); max take-off 5,060 lb (2295 kg)
Dimensions: span 31 ft 9⅞ in (9.70 m); length 27 ft 0⅞ in (8.26 m); height 10 ft 0⅜ in (3.05 m); wing area 241.1 sq ft (22.40 m²)
Armament: two 12.7-mm (0.5-in) Breda SAFAT machine-guns in nose (some aircraft also with two 12.7-mm/0.5-in guns under lower wing); two 220-lb (100-kg) bombs

Fiat G.50 Freccia

Sporting the 'cat and mice' emblem of the 56° Stormo CT, this G.50bis was one of the Belgium-based Italian aircraft at the end of the Battle of Britain. The Freccia squadrons seemed to have successfully evaded combat with the RAF.

Giuseppe Gabrielli's **G.50 Freccia** (Arrow) fighter was designed in 1935-36, and offered less in operational potential than the contemporary Hawker Hurricane and Messerschmitt Bf 109. The prototype G.50 first flew on 26 February 1937 and was the first Regia Aeronautica all-metal monoplane with constant-speed propeller and retractable landing gear. The G.50 was ordered into production with the CMASA company (a subsidiary of Fiat) and 12 of the first aircraft were sent to Spain for operational evaluation. Despite the superiority of the Macchi C.200, one *stormo* and one *gruppo* were equipped with the G.50, and an initial order for 200 aircraft was placed. In November 1939 the type was delivered to the 51° Stormo, and soon afterwards to the 52° Stormo, and when Italy entered the war in the following June 118 Freccias were in service. In November 1940, 48 G.50s of the 51° Stormo moved to Belgium to take part in the air attacks on the UK; however, they saw little action, being principally engaged in 'surveillance' duties. In September that year the prototype of a new version, the **G.50bis**, had flown, and with improved cockpit armour and increased fuel this entered production for eventual service with five *gruppi* in North Africa. With a maximum speed of only 286 mph (460 km/h) and an armament of two machine-guns, the G.50 was hardly a match for RAF fighters, yet it served until July 1943. Production reached 245 G.50 and 421 G.50bis fighters, and 108 of a dual-control two-seat trainer, the **G.50B**. G.50s also went to Croatian and Finnish air forces.

Fiat G.50bis Freccia

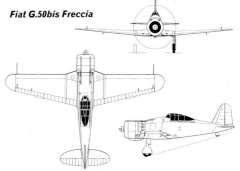

Specification: Fiat G.50 Freccia
Type: single-seat fighter
Powerplant: one 840-hp (627-kW) Fiat A.74 RC 38 radial piston
Performance: max speed 286 mph (460 km/h) at 13,125 ft (4000 m); climb to 13,125 ft (4000 m) in 4.6 minutes; service ceiling 35,270 ft (10750 m); range 360 miles (580 km)
Weights: empty 4,332 lb (1965 kg); max take-off 5,291 lb (2400 kg)
Dimensions: span 36 ft 0½ in (11.00 m); length 25 ft 7 in (7.80 m); height 10 ft 9¼ in (3.28 m); wing area 196.45 sq ft (18.25 m²)
Armament: two nose-mounted 12.7-mm (0.5-in) Breda SAFAT machine-guns

Handicapped by the lack of a suitable inline engine, Italian fighters at the beginning of the war had to make do with bulky radials. The Fiat G.50 in particular had a disappointing performance.

Focke-Wulf Fw 190

This Fw 190A-8 belonged to I./JG 1, based at Twenthe in the Netherlands in December 1944. The red stripe around the fuselage is a Defence of the Reich band.

The 1937 **Focke-Wulf Fw 190** featured a bulky air-cooled BMW radial engine. First flown on 1 June 1939, the prototype was followed by short- and long-span pre-production **Fw 190A-0**s, with BMW 801 14-cylinder radials (the latter selected for production). **Fw 190A-1**s joined the Luftwaffe in mid-1941 and proved superior to the Spitfire Mk V. A-series variants included the **Fw 190A-3** with BMW 801D-2 and two 7.92-mm (0.31-in) and four 20-mm guns, and the **Fw 190A-4** with water-methanol power-boosting (with fighter-bomber, bomber-destroyer and tropicalised sub-variants). The **Fw 190A-5** featured a lengthened nose, and sub-variants included versions with six 30-mm guns (**A-5/U12**) and torpedo-fighters (**A-5/U14** and **U15**). 1943's **Fw 190A-7** and **Fw 190A-8** had increased armament and armour. The **Fw 190A-8/U1** was a two-seat conversion trainer. The **Fw 190D** featured a lengthened nose and Jumo 213 inline engine in annular cowling. The **Fw 190D-9** joined the Luftwaffe in 1944, and was regarded as Germany's best piston-engined fighter; it had a top speed of 426 mph (685 km/h), was armed with two cannon and two machine-guns, and was powered by a water-methanol boosted 2,240-hp (1671-kW) Jumo 2213A. The **Fw 190F** and **Fw 190G** fighter-bombers carried 2,205 lb (1000 kg) of bombs. The long-span **Ta 152** (Fw 190D development) had increased armament and Jumo 213E/B (top speed 472 mph/760 km/h at 41,010 ft/12500 m), some reaching the Luftwaffe before the end of the war.

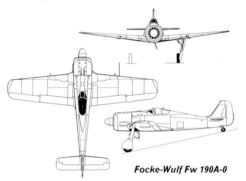

Focke-Wulf Fw 190A-0

This Focke-Wulf Fw 190G-2 ground attack variant is equipped with a centreline ETC 250 bomb rack capable of mounting a single 551-lb (250-kg) bomb. Other versions of the Fw 190G could carry bomb loads of up to 3,970 lb (1800 kg).

Specification: Focke-Wulf Fw 190A-8
Type: single-seat fighter
Powerplant: one 2,100-hp (1567-kW) BMW 801D-2 radial piston with water-methanol boosting
Performance: max speed 408 mph (654 km/h) at 19,685 ft (6000 m); initial climb rate 2,362 ft (720 m) per minute; service ceiling 37,400 ft (11400 m); normal range 500 miles (805 km)
Weights: empty 6,989 lb (3170 kg); max take-off 10,802 lb (4900 kg)
Dimensions: span 34 ft 5½ in (10.50 m); length 29 ft 1½ in (8.84 m); height 13 ft 0 in (3.96 m); wing area 196.98 sq ft (18.30 m²)
Armament: two 7.92-mm (0.31-in) guns on nose, up to four 20-mm guns in wings; wide range of underfuselage/wing bombs, guns and rockets

Focke-Wulf Fw 200 Condor

Displaying the ringed globe insignia of I./KG 40 (recalling the long-distance flights by commercial Condors), this Fw 200 of 1. Staffel was based at Bordeaux-Merignac late in 1940.

A pre-war airliner with many long-distance flights and records, the four-engined **Focke-Wulf Fw 200 Condor** was designed by Kurt Tank in 1936, and underwent adaptation into a potent anti-shipping aircraft with the Luftwaffe. Ten pre-production **Fw 200C-0** maritime reconnaissance aircraft were delivered in September 1939, some serving with I./KG 40 in 1940. Five-crew production **Fw 200C-1s** had four 830-hp (619-kW) BMW 132H engines and could carry four 551-lb (250-kg) bombs. Apart from long-range maritime patrols over the Atlantic, the Fw 200C-1s also undertook extensive minelaying in British waters during 1940, each carrying two 2,205-lb (1000-kg) mines. Numerous sub-variants of the C series appeared, the **Fw 200C-3** with 1,000-hp (746-kW) Bramo 323R-2 radials being the most important. Later in the war the **Fw 200C-6** and **Fw 200C-8** were produced in an effort to enhance the Condor's operational potential by adaptation to carry two Henschel Hs 293 missiles in conjunction with FuG 203b missile control radio. Rugged operating conditions highlighted the Fw 200's weaknesses and there were many service accidents. In the mid-war years Fw 200s were employed briefly as military transports, 18 aircraft being flown by Kampfgruppe zur besonderen Venwendung 200 in support of the beleaguered German forces at Stalingrad. Other Condors were used by Hitler and Himmler as personal transports. Focke-Wulf Fw 200 production for the Luftwaffe amounted to 252 aircraft between 1940 and 1944.

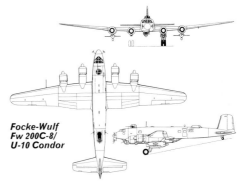

Focke-Wulf Fw 200C-8/ U-10 Condor

Specification: Focke-Wulf Fw 200C-3/U4
Type: seven-crew maritime reconnaissance bomber
Powerplant: four 1,000-hp (746-kW) BMW-Bramo 323R-2 radial pistons
Performance: max speed 224 mph (360 km/h) at 15,420 ft (4700 m); service ceiling 19,685 ft (6000 m); range 2,211 miles (3560 km)
Weight: empty 37,478 lb (17000 kg); max take-off 50,044 lb (22700 kg)
Dimensions: span 107 ft 9½ in (32.84 m); length 76 ft 11½ in (23.85 m); height 20 ft 8 in (6.30 m); wing area 1,290.0 sq ft (118.00 m²)
Armament: forward dorsal 7.92-mm (0.31-in) gun, rear dorsal 13-mm (0.51-in) gun, two beam 13-mm (0.51-in) guns, ventral 20-mm gun, aft ventral 7.92-mm (0.31-in) gun; max bomb load 4,630 lb (2100 kg)

The Focke-Wulf Fw 200 originated in a pre-war long-range commercial airliner. The Fw 200C-1, seen here, was armed with a 20-mm gun in the nose and three 7.92-mm (0.31-in) guns in other positions.

Gloster Gladiator

Despite being obsolescent, Gloster Gladiators saw service first in France and then Norway, and were even available in small numbers as a back-up in the Battle of Britain. This example is Belgian.

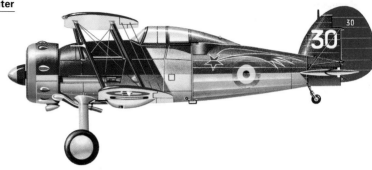

By 1939, the **Gloster Gladiator** was obsolescent and scheduled for replacement as a front-line RAF fighter. The exigencies of the wartime situation meant that the type was retained. Production of the Gladiator **Mk I** amounted to 378 aircraft, all powered by the 840-hp (627-kW) Bristol Mercury IX radial pioneered in the prototype, which had first flown in September 1934. The Gladiator served with seven RAF squadrons in northern Europe. As was common practice in the RAF, the obsolescent Gladiator was relegated to secondary theatres, notably North Africa, and here the type was the most modern fighter available to meet the Italians when the latter entered the war in June 1940. The type fought with considerable distinction over the Western Desert up to 1942, and was also gainfully employed in the Maltese and Greek campaigns. The principal wartime variant was the **Mk II**, essentially a Mk I with the 840-hp (627-kW) Mercury VIIA or Mercury VIIAS. The aircraft intended for operations in North Africa had tropical equipment, and six North African squadrons were equipped with the type. The other British version was the **Sea Gladiator**, which had catapult points,

an arrester hook and dinghy stowage. Production amounted to 60 aircraft, supplemented by 38 Mk IIs converted as **Interim Sea Gladiators**. A considerable number of Gladiators were exported, and 18 aircraft were operated by Sweden under the designation **J8A** with Nohab Mercury VIIIS.3 radials.

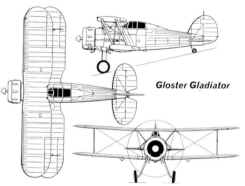

Gloster Gladiator

At the time of Italy's entry into the war in June 1940, the defence of Malta – strategically vital to Britain in the Mediterranean – rested solely on a handful of Sea Gladiators, kept there as fleet replacements. Piloted by volunteers, they sought to defend the island from half-hearted attacks by the Italian air force.

Specification: Gloster Gladiator Mk II
Type: single-seat interceptor fighter
Powerplant: one 840-hp (627-kW) Bristol Mercury VIIIA radial piston
Performance: max speed 255 mph (410 km/h) at 14,500 ft (4420 m); initial climb rate 2,300 ft (701 m) per minute; service ceiling 33,000 ft (10060 m); range 440 miles (708 km)
Weights: empty 3,480 lb (1570 kg); max take-off 4,810 lb (2182 kg)
Dimensions: span 32 ft 3 in (9.83 m); length 27 ft 5 in (8.36 m); height 11 ft 9 in (3.63 m); wing area 323.0 sq ft (30.01 m²)
Armament: two 0.303-in (7.7-mm) Browning machine-guns in nose and two 0.303-in (7.7-mm) Browning or Vickers guns under lower wings

Gotha Go 242

This Gotha Go 244B wears the markings of 4./KGrzbV 106 early in 1943. By this time, however, the unit had almost entirely re-equipped with the Junkers Ju 52/3m.

Designed by Albert Kalkert, the **Gotha Go 242** transport and assault glider was the most widely used operational glider in the Luftwaffe's wartime arsenal between 1942 and 1945, and was employed in the Balkans, Sicily, North Africa and, of course, on the Eastern Front. The first glider flew in early 1941, and was developed into the **Go 242A** production aircraft, followed by the **Go 242B** with a nosewheel. During Go 242 development, consideration had been given to motorising the glider, including the addition of a single engine on the nose to maintain altitude after a towed launch. After the fall of France, the French Gnome-Rhône 14M radial engine became available to the Germans in large numbers, and the Go 242 was modified to serve as the **Go 244** twin-engined transport, each of the twin booms being extended forward of the leading edge of the wing to mount one of these engines; at the same time, fixed tricycle landing gear was installed. A total of 133 conversions was made from the five Go 242B variants, being designated correspondingly **Go 244B-1** to **B-5**. First deliveries were made in March 1942 to the Greece-based KGrzbV 104 and to KGrzbV 106

in Crete, but they proved to be underpowered and relatively easy targets for Allied fighter aircraft, and had been withdrawn by November 1942 and distributed to paratroop training schools. Some Go 244s had 660-hp (492-kW) BMW 132Z, or captured Shvetsov M-25As each of 750 hp (559 kW).

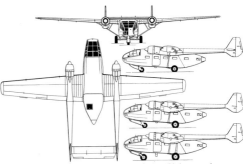

Gotha Go 244B-1 (upper view: Go 224V, lower view: Go 244B-2)

Specification: Gotha Go 244B-2
Powerplant: two 700-hp (522-kW) Gnome-Rhône 14M 14-cylinder radial pistons
Performance: max speed 180 mph (290 km/h); service ceiling 24,605 ft (7500 m); range 373 miles (600 km)
Weights: empty 11,243 lb (5100 kg); max take-off 17,196 lb (7800 kg)
Dimensions: span 80 ft 4½ in (24.50 m); length 51 ft 10 in (15.80 m); height 15 ft 5 in (4.70 m); wing area 693.22 sq ft (64.40 m²)
Armament: four 0.31-in (7.92-mm) MG 15 machine-guns

Gotha Go 244 powered glider. Some 133 gliders were converted to the powered Go 244 version with 700-hp (522-kW) Gnome-Rhône 14M radial engines. When flown in North Africa, aircraft of this type were very vulnerable to anti-aircraft fire and were quickly withdrawn.

Grumman F4F Wildcat

This Grumman Wildcat Mk VI belonged to the Fleet Air Arm. The General Motors-built variant (equivalent to the US Navy's FM-2) could be identified by the taller fin, necessary to cope with the increased power of the Wright R-1820 engine.

When first flown on 2 September 1937, the **Grumman XF4F-2** single-seat naval fighter prototype was underpowered. With a two-stage supercharged XR-1830-76 fitted, a speed of 333.5 mph (537 km/h) was recorded during US Navy trials with the **XF4F-3**. Fifty-four **F4F-3**s were ordered in August 1939, 22 of which had been delivered by the end of 1940. These aircraft served with VF-4 and VF-7 and were followed by 95 **F4F-3A**s with single-stage supercharged R-1830-90s. France in 1939 ordered 81 Wildcats which were transferred to the UK, serving with the Royal Navy as the **Martlet**. US Navy and Marine Corps F4Fs were heavily engaged during the early months of the war with the Japanese, numerous aircraft being destroyed on the ground, but also scoring a number of victories. The **F4F-4** (1,169 produced), with manually-folding wings, was delivered during 1942, and an unarmed long-range reconnaissance version of this, the **F4F-7**, had a range of over 3,500 miles (5633 km). The F4F-4 was also built by General Motors as the **FM-1**, as was a more powerful version, the **FM-2**, for operation from escort carriers. FM-1s and -2s were supplied to the UK as the **Wildcat Mk V** and **Mk VI** (the name Martlet was dropped). F4F-4s were heavily committed in the battles of Midway and the Coral Sea. Production of the Wildcat (excluding prototypes) totalled 7,885, including 5,237 FM-1s and FM-2s by General Motors, and 1,100 for the UK.

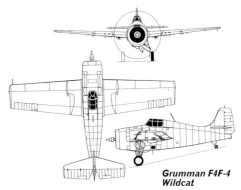

Grumman F4F-4 Wildcat

A contemporary of the Japanese Zero-Sen naval fighter, the F4F Wildcat was somewhat inferior in performance, but usually held its own largely owing to its heavier armament. Although obsolete in the last two years of the war, the Wildcat, on account of its small folded size, continued to fly from small escort carriers.

Specification:
Grumman F4F-4 Wildcat
Type: single-seat shipboard fighter
Powerplant: one 1,200-hp (895-kW) Pratt & Whitney R-1830-86 radial piston
Performance: max speed 318 mph (512 km/h) at 19,400 ft (5915 m); initial climb rate 1,950 ft (594 m) per minute; service ceiling 34,900 ft (1064.0 m); range 770 miles (1240 km)
Weights: empty 5,785 lb (2624 kg); max take-off 7,952 lb (3607 kg)
Dimensions: span 38 ft 0 in (11.58 m); length 28 ft 9 in (8.76 m); height 11 ft 10 in (3.60 m); wing area 260.0 sq ft (24.15 m²)
Armament: six forward-firing 0.5-in (12.7-mm) guns; FM-2 had four guns and provision to carry two 250-lb (113-kg) bombs or six 5-in (127-mm) rockets

Grumman F6F Hellcat

For an aircraft that only entered service two years before the war's end, the production total of 12,275 Hellcats was a remarkable achievement. In the same period it destroyed 4,947 enemy aircraft – excluding those shot down by British pilots of the Fleet Air Arm.

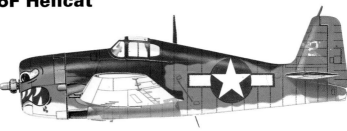

One of America's best wartime shipboard fighters, and second only to the F4U Corsair, the **Grumman F6F Hellcat** was the logical development of the F4F Wildcat. It was first flown as the **XF6F-3** on 26 June 1942, production **F6F-3**s following only five weeks later. Deliveries to VF-9 aboard USS *Essex* started early in 1943, and night-fighter versions comprised the **F6F-3E** and **F6F-3N** with radar in a wing pod. In 1944 the **F6F-5** appeared with provision for 2,000 lb (907 kg) of bombs and with two 20-mm cannon sometimes replacing the inboard wing 0.5-in (12.7-mm) guns. The radar-equipped night-fighter version was the **F6F-5N**. Production totalled 6,435 F6F-5s and 1,189 F6F-5Ns, while 252 F6F-3s and 930 F6F-5s served with the British Fleet Air Arm as the **Hellcat Mk I** and **Mk II**, respectively. Production of all F6Fs amounted to 12,275, and official figures credited the US Navy and Marine Corps aircraft with the destruction of 5,156 enemy aircraft in air combat, about 75 per cent of all the US Navy's air combat victories in the war. The Hellcat's most impressive victory was in that greatest of all carrier battles, the Battle of the Philippine Sea, in which 15 American

aircraft-carriers embarked 480 F6F fighters (plus 222 dive-bombers and 199 torpedo-bombers); by the end of a week's fighting Task Force 58 had destroyed more than 400 Japanese aircraft and sunk three carriers. Hellcats were still serving with the US Navy several years after the war.

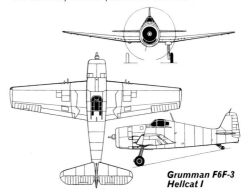

Grumman F6F-3 Hellcat I

Specification:
Grumman F6F-5 Hellcat
Type: single-seat shipboard fighter
Powerplant: one 2,000-hp (1492-kW) Pratt & Whitney R-2800-10W radial piston
Performance: max speed 380 mph (612 km/h) at 23,400 ft (7130 m); initial climb rate 2,980 ft (908 m) per minute; service ceiling 37,300 ft (11370 m); range 945 miles (1529 km)
Weights: empty 9,238 lb (4190 kg); max take-off 15,413 lb (6991 kg)
Dimensions: span 42 ft 10 in (13.05 m); length 33 ft 7 in (10.23 m); height 13 ft 1 in (3.99 m); wing area 334.0 sq ft (31.03 m²)
Armament: six 0.5-in (12.7-mm) machine-guns in wings, or two 20-mm cannon and four 0.5-in (12.7-mm) guns in wings; two 1,000-lb (454-kg) bombs

This Grumman F6F-3 wears the red-bordered US Navy markings used between July and September 1943. This was the initial production version of the Hellcat and first saw action with US Navy Squadron VF-5 from the carrier USS Essex *on 31 August 1943, in the Pacific.*

Grumman TBF Avenger

The Avenger possessed all the characteristics inherent in American wartime naval aircraft: compactness, strength, and good performance. The type eventually became the US Navy's standard torpedo-bomber in the Pacific.

Destined to become one of the best shipborne torpedo-bombers of the war, the **Grumman TBF Avenger** initially saw combat during the great Battle of Midway. The **XTBF-1** prototype was first flown on 1 August 1941 after an order for 286 aircraft had already been placed. The first **TBF-1**s appeared in January 1942 and VT-8 ('Torpedo Eight') received its first aircraft during the following May. On 4 June, six of VT-8's aircraft were launched at the height of the Battle of Midway, but only one returned – and this with one gunner dead and the other wounded. Despite this inauspicious start, production accelerated as General Motors undertook production in addition to Grumman, producing the **TBM-1** version. Sub-variants included the **TBF-1C** with two 20-mm cannon in the wings, the **TBF-1B** which was supplied to the UK under Lend-Lease, the **TBF-1D** and **TBF-1E** with ASV radar, and the **TBF-1L** with a searchlight in the bomb bay. Production of the TBF-1 and TBM-1, as well as sub-variants, totalled 2,290 and 2,882, respectively. General Motors (Eastern Division) went on to produce 4,664 **TBM-3**s with R-2600-20 engines, and the sub-variants corresponded with those of the TBF-1s. The UK received 395 **TBF-1B**s and 526 **TBM-3B**s, and New Zealand took 63. The **TBM-3P** camera-equipped aircraft and the **TBM-3H** with search radar were the final wartime versions. The Avenger served with the US Navy until 1954.

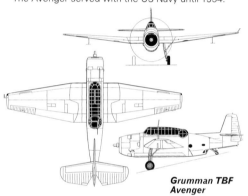

Grumman TBF Avenger

The Grumman TBF Avenger arrived in service just in time to participate in the Battle of Midway on 4 June 1942. These TBF-1s are from No. 846 Squadron, Royal Navy.

Specification: Grumman (General Motors) TBM-3E Avenger
Type: three-crew shipborne torpedo-bomber
Powerplant: one 1,900-hp (1417-kW) Wright R-2600-20 radial piston
Performance: max speed 276 mph (444 km/h) at 16,500 ft (5030 m); climb rate 2,060 ft (628 m) per minute; ceiling 30,100 ft (9175 m); range 1,010 miles (1625 km)
Weights: empty 10,545 lb (4783 kg); max take-off 17,895 lb (8117 kg)
Dimensions: span 54 ft 2 in (16.51 m); length 40 ft 11½ in (12.48 m); height 15 ft 5 in (4.70 m); wing area 490.0 sq ft (45.52 m²)
Armament: two fixed forward-firing 0.5-in (12.7-mm) guns, dorsal 0.5-in (12.7-mm) gun, ventral 0.3-in (7.62-mm) gun; 2,000 lb (907 kg) bombs, or one torpedo

Handley Page Halifax

Sporting the distinctive tail marking adopted by squadrons of Bomber Command's No. 4 Group, this Halifax Mk III of No. 466 Sqn, RAAF, was based at Leconfield in the mid-war years.

Second only in importance to the Avro Lancaster in Bomber Command's great night offensive of 1941-1945, the four-engined **Handley Page Halifax** was originally designed around a pair of Vulture engines but, when first flown on 25 October 1939, the choice of four Merlins had been made. The first aircraft arrived on No. 35 Squadron in November 1940 and flew their first raid on 10-11 March 1941. Production was widely sub-contracted and quickly accelerated, the Merlin X-powered Halifax **Mk I** with two-gun nose turret and no dorsal turret being followed by the **Mk IIA Series I** with Merlin XX and two-gun dorsal turret. In the Halifax **Mk II Series I (Special)** the nose turret was omitted, and in the **Mk II Series IA** a large transparent fairing improved the whole nose shape, this version also introducing a Defiant-type four-gun dorsal turret. The Halifax **Mk III** was powered by Bristol Hercules XVI radials, and later examples introduced a wingspan increased from 98 ft 10 in (30.12 m) to 104 ft 2 in (31.75 m). The **Mk V** with Dowty landing gear served with Coastal and Bomber Commands; the **Mk VI** with Hercules 100 engines and **Mk VII** with Hercules XVI (both versions with increased fuel capacity) joined Bomber Command in 1944. Halifax Mk III, V and VII versions also served in paratrooping and glider-towing roles with the airborne forces (being the only aircraft to tow the big Hamilcar) and were joined by the **Mk VIII** just before the end of the war. Production totalled 6,176 Halifaxes, the bomber versions flying a total of 75,532 sorties and dropping 227,610 tons of bombs.

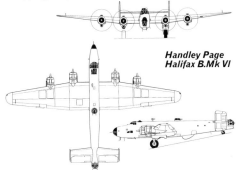

Handley Page Halifax B.Mk VI

Specification: Handley Page Halifax Mk VI
Type: seven-crew night heavy bomber
Powerplant: four 1,800-hp (1343-kW) Bristol Hercules 100 radial pistons
Performance: max speed 312 mph (502 km/h) at 22,000 ft (6705 m); climb to 20,000 ft (6095 m) in 5.0 minutes; ceiling 24,000 ft (7315 m); range with 13,000-lb (5897-kg) bomb load 1,260 miles (2028 km)
Weights: empty 39,000 lb (17,690 kg); max take-off 68,000 lb (30845 kg)
Dimensions: span 104 ft 2 in (31.75 m); length 71 ft 7 in (21.82 m); height 20 ft 9 in (6.32 m); wing area 1,275.0 sq ft (118.45 m²)
Armament: 0.303-in (7.7-mm) gun in nose, four 0.303-in (7.7-mm) guns in dorsal and tail turrets; max bomb load 13,000 lb (5897 kg)

Second of the RAF's four-engined heavy bombers to enter service (after the Stirling), the Halifax was originally powered by Rolls-Royce Merlin engines but, with Hercules radials, served with Bomber Command until the end of the war. A Halifax Mk II of No. 35 Squadron is shown here.

Handley Page Hampden

Pictured here is a Hampden Mk I of No. 420 (Snowy Owl) Sqn, RCAF, based at Waddington, Lincs. This squadron's first operation was an attack by five aircraft on Emden on the night of 21/22 January 1942.

The only RAF medium bomber at the beginning of the war to lack power-operated defensive gun turrets, the **Handley Page Hampden** was nevertheless widely used by Bomber Command during the first three years. Designed to a 1932 specification, it was first flown on 21 June 1936 and joined No. 49 Squadron in August 1938. At the war's beginning the Hampden **Mk I** equipped eight squadrons. (A Napier Dagger-powered version, the Hereford, of which 101 were built, was used almost exclusively as an aircrew trainer.) In due course, a total of 15 Bomber Command squadrons flew Hampden Mk Is, taking part in many of the epic early war raids, during which two VCs were awarded (to Flight Lieutenant R. A. B. Learoyd of No. 49 Squadron and to Sergeant J. Hannah of No. 83 Squadron). Although possessing a fairly good speed, the Hampden proved to be very vulnerable in the presence of enemy night-fighters and was withdrawn as an operational bomber after its last raid on 14-15 September 1942. Four Coastal Command squadrons were then equipped with Hampden torpedo-bombers, two of them (Nos 144 and 255) being based for a short time near

Murmansk for protection of the North Cape convoys; the others operated against enemy shipping in the North Sea. Three other squadrons were employed for weather reconnaissance by Coastal Command. The Wright Cyclone-powered Hampden **Mk II** did not enter production. Hampden production totalled 1,270 in Britain and 160 in Canada.

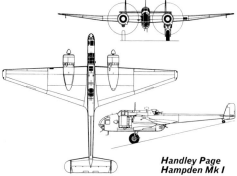

Handley Page Hampden Mk I

Widely used by Bomber Command during the first years of the war, the Hampden was the only member of the so-called heavy bombers of that period that was not equipped with any power-operated gun turret. With only hand-held guns for tail defence, the aircraft was particularly vulnerable in the presence of night-fighters.

Specification: Handley Page Hampden Mk I
Type: four-crew medium bomber
Powerplant: two 1,000-hp (746-kW) Bristol Pegasus XVIII radial pistons
Performance: max speed 254 mph (409 km/h) at 13,800 ft (4205 m); climb rate 980 ft (299 m) per minute; ceiling 19,000 ft (5790 m); range with 4,000-lb (1814-kg) bomb load 1,200 miles (1931 km)
Weights: empty 11,780 lb (5343 kg); max take-off 21,000 lb (9526 kg)
Dimensions: span 69 ft 2 in (21.08 m); length 53 ft 7 in (16.33 m); height 14 ft 11 in (4.55 m); wing area 688.0 sq ft (63.92 m²)
Armament: one fixed and one flexible 0.303-in (7.7-mm) gun in nose, twin 0.303-in (7.7-mm) guns in dorsal and ventral positions; max bomb load 4,000 lb (1814 kg)

Hawker Hurricane

The Hurricane was the first monoplane fighter and the first with a top speed of over 300 mph (483 km/h) to enter RAF service. This Mk I is from No. 85 Sqn, which was based at Debden and Croydon in August 1940.

Sydney Camm's **Hawker Hurricane** first flew on 6 November 1935 and joined the RAF in December 1937. The **Mk I** with 1,030-hp (768-kW) Rolls-Royce Merlin II and an armament of eight 0.303-in (7.7-mm) machine-guns was Fighter Command's principal fighter in the Battle of Britain in 1940, and destroyed more enemy aircraft than all other defences combined. The **Mk IIA** with 1,280-hp (955-kW) Merlin XX followed before the end of 1940, the **Mk IIB** with 12 machine-guns and the **Mk IIC** with four 20-mm cannon during 1941. These versions were also able to carry up to two 500-lb (227-kg) bombs, drop tanks or other stores under the wings; they served as fighters, fighter-bombers, night-fighters, intruders and photo-reconnaissance aircraft on all fronts until 1943, and in the Far East until the end of the war. In 1942 the **Mk IID** introduced the 40-mm anti-tank gun (two carried under the wings), this version being quite successful in North Africa. The **Mk IV** featured a 'universal wing' which allowed carriage of up to eight 60-lb (27.2-kg) rocket projectiles or any of the external stores carried by the Mk II. Over 14,000 Hurricanes were produced, with 1,451 **Mks X, XI** and **XII** built in Canada. This total included many **Sea Hurricanes**, of which early versions were catapulted from merchant ships and flown from converted merchant aircraft-carriers, and later served aboard RN fleet carriers.

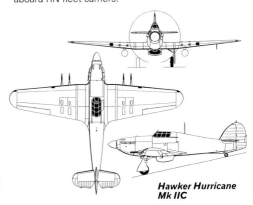

Hawker Hurricane Mk IIC

Specification: Hawker Hurricane Mk IIC
Type: single-seat fighter and fighter-bomber
Powerplant: one 1,280-hp (955-kW) Rolls-Royce Merlin XX inline piston
Performance: max speed 336 mph (541 km/h) at 12,500 ft (3810 m); climb to 20,000 ft (6095 m) in 9.1 minutes; ceiling 35,600 ft (10850 m); range on internal fuel 460 miles (740 km)
Weights: empty 5,800 lb (2631 kg); loaded 8,100 lb (3674 kg)
Dimensions: span 40 ft 0 in (12.19 m); length 32 ft 0 in (9.75 m); height 13 ft 1 in (3.99 m); wing area 257.5 sq ft (23.92 m²)
Armament: four 20-mm wing cannon; two 500-lb (227-kg) bombs, or eight 60-lb (27.2-kg) rocket projectiles or two 90-Imp gal (409-litre) drop tanks under wings

A Hurricane Mk IIC night-fighter of No. 87 Sqn. Armed with four 20-mm cannon, this version performed freelance night intruder missions over France in the mid-war years and, although without the benefit of airborne radar, gained many victories in the skies over enemy bomber bases.

Hawker Tempest

The Tempest was an improved version of the Typhoon, featuring a laminar-flow elliptical wing and a lengthened fuselage to accommodate additional fuel. This aircraft is a Tempest Mk V.

Conscious that the Typhoon left much to be desired as an interceptor fighter as soon as it flew in 1940, Sydney Camm initiated the development of the **Hawker Tempest**. This aircraft was first flown on 2 September 1942 and was followed by production Tempest **Mk V**s, which joined Nos 3 and 486 Squadrons in April 1944. The early aircraft, Tempest **Mk V Series 1**s, were armed with four long-barrelled 20-mm Hispano Mk II cannon, but **Mk V Series 2**s featured improved short-barrelled Mk V guns. Tempests were first committed to combat when the German flying-bomb offensive opened immediately after the Normandy landings, and the type shot down 638 out of the RAF's total of 1,771 bombs destroyed. Meanwhile, like the Typhoon, Tempests were being employed in the ground-attack role, being equipped to carry up to two 1,000-lb (454-kg) bombs, drop tanks or eight 60-lb (27.2-kg) rocket projectiles. With its top speed of 426 mph (686 km/h), the Tempest also proved an effective fighter against the new German aircraft then being introduced, and there were several instances of their shooting down Messerschmitt Me 262 jet fighters. The Mk V equipped 12 wartime RAF squadrons, 800 aircraft being completed (and 1,200 cancelled at the end of the war). The superb Bristol Centaurus-powered **Mk II**, although flying well before the end of hostilities, was too late to see action and was intended for service in the Far East.

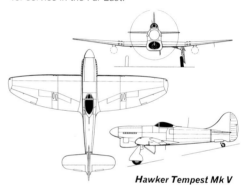

Hawker Tempest Mk V

Arguably the best single-seat fighter produced for the RAF during the war, the Hawker Tempest Mk V was much in evidence in the defence against the flying bombs of 1944. In the final months of the war it also served in the ground attack role on the continent.

Specification: Hawker Tempest Mk V
Type: single-seat interceptor/ground attack fighter
Powerplant: one 2,180-hp (1626-kW) Napier Sabre II inline piston
Performance: max speed 426 mph (685 km/h) at 18,500 ft (5660 m); climb to 15,000 ft (4570 m) in 5.0 minutes; ceiling 38,000 ft (11580 m); range on internal fuel 740 miles (1190 km)
Weights: empty 9,000 lb (4082 kg); max take-off 13,540 lb (6142 kg)
Dimensions: span 41 ft 0 in (12.50 m); length 33 ft 8 in (10.26 m); height 16 ft 1 in (4.90 m); wing area 302.0 sq ft (28.06 m²)
Armament: four 20-mm cannon in wings; two 1,000-lb (454-kg) bombs, or eight 60-lb (27.2-kg) 3-in (7.62 cm) rocket projectiles, napalm or long-range fuel tanks

Hawker Typhoon

This late production Typhoon Mk IB of No. 440 Sqn, RCAF, was based at Goch during the final Allied advance into Germany. The aircraft is shown with a pair of 1,000-lb (454-kg) bombs.

Conceived as a Hurricane replacement, the **Hawker Typhoon** entered the design process in 1937 around the new Napier Sabre 24-cylinder H-type inline engine (in parallel with the Hawker Tornado with Rolls-Royce Vulture engine). First flown on 24 February 1940, the Typhoon underwent accelerated development, as did its engine, and entered service with Nos 56 and 609 Squadrons in September 1941, the Tornado having been abandoned because of difficulties with the Vulture. The Typhoon **Mk IA** was armed with 12 0.303-in (7.7-mm) machine-guns in the wings, and the **Mk IB** with four 20-mm cannon. Rushed development resulted in numerous accidents (caused by a structural weakness in the rear fuselage and a spate of engine failures) and after a short time the Typhoon was withdrawn from normal interception duties, being confined to the low-level interceptor role, and eventually ground attack, a duty for which the big fighter was particularly well suited. In 1943 the aircraft was flown with two 500-lb (227-kg) bombs under the wings, and the following year its load was increased to two 1,000-lb (454-kg) bombs or drop tanks or, most successfully, to eight 60-lb

(27.2-kg) rocket projectiles. During the final year of the European war the rocket-firing **Mk IB** proved to be one of the most effective ground support fighters, called on to attack enemy targets and doing so with devastating effect during the Allied advance across northern Europe from Normandy.

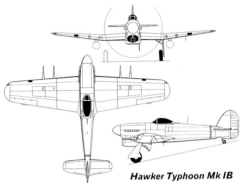

Hawker Typhoon Mk IB

Specification: Hawker Typhoon Mk IB
Type: single-seat fighter-bomber
Powerplant: one 2,180-hp (1626-kW) Napier Sabre II inline piston
Performance: max speed 405 mph (652 km/h) at 18,000 ft (5485 m); climb to 15,000 ft (4570 m) in 6.2 minutes; service ceiling 34,000 ft (10365 m); range with two 1,000-lb (454-kg) bombs 510 miles (821 km)
Weights: empty 8,800 lb (3992 kg); max take-off 13,980 lb (6341 kg)
Dimensions: span 41 ft 7 in (12.67 m); length 31 ft 11 in (9.74 m); height 15 ft 3½ in (4.67 m); wing area 279.0 sq ft (25.92 m²)
Armament: four wing 20-mm cannon; two 1,000-lb (454-kg) bombs or eight 60-lb (27.2-kg) 3-in (7.62-cm) rocket projectiles under wings

Rugged, powerful and fast, the Typhoon was certainly a handful for its pilots but proved a devastating weapon in the ground attack role. A total of 3,330 aircraft was built, eventually equipping 32 squadrons of the RAF. Here, ground crew prepare a Typhoon Mk IB of No. 175 Sqn for a bombing sortie.

Heinkel He 111

This Heinkel He 111H-3 belonged to 1./KG 54 'Totenkopf', which operated in the opening phases of the May 1940 campaign over France, Belgium and the Netherlands. This aircraft with its Death's Head unit badge flew from Delmenhorst.

The **Heinkel He 111** stemmed from a design for a dual-purpose commercial transport bomber produced in 1934 and flown on 24 February 1935. Early versions featured conventional stepped windscreen and elliptical wing leading edge, and a bomber version with these features (**He 111B-1**) served in the Spanish Civil War. The first production version with straight wing leading edge was the **He 111F**, and the **He 111P** incorporated a fully-glazed asymmetric nose without external windscreen step. He 111Ps with DB 601Aa engines were delivered in 1939 before production switched to the most widely-used variant, the **He 111H** with Junkers Jumo 211 engines; sub-variants of this series formed the backbone of the bomber force between 1940 and 1943, when they took part in numerous raids in the Battle of Britain and were flown by the pathfinder unit, KGr 100. First to carry torpedoes was the **He 111H-6**, followed by the **He 111H-15**; the **He 111H-8** was fitted with a large balloon cable fender; the **He 111H-11/R2** was a glider tug for the Go 242; pathfinder versions with special radio were the **He 111H-14** and **He 111H-18**; the **He 111H-16** featured increased gun arma-

ment; and the **He 111H-20** included 16-paratroop transport, night bomber and glider tug sub-variants. The **He 111H-22** carried a single Fi 103 flying bomb and was used against the UK late in 1944. Most extraordinary was the **He 111Z Zwilling** (Twin), two He 111Hs joined with a new wing and fifth engine and used to tow the Me 321 Gigant gliders.

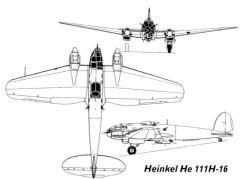

Heinkel He 111H-16

Among the bomber units switched from the night assault on Britain to the Eastern Front in 1941 was KG 55 'Greif' (Griffon wing), one of whose Heinkel He 111Hs is seen here being armed prior to a raid. A total of about 7,300 He 111s was built, the type being the longest-serving Luftwaffe medium bomber.

Specification: Heinkel He 111H-16
Type: five-crew bomber
Powerplant: two 1,350-hp (1007-kW) Junkers Jumo 211F inline pistons
Performance: max speed 271 km/h (436 mph) at 19,685 ft (6000 m); climb to 19,685 ft (6000 m) in 42.0 minutes; ceiling 21,980 ft (6700 m); range 1,212 miles (1950 km)
Weights: empty 19,136 lb (8680 kg); max take-off 30,865 lb (14000 kg)
Dimensions: span 74 ft 1¾ in (22.60 m); length 53 ft 9½ in (16.40 m); height 13 ft 1¼ in (3.40 m); wing area 931.07 sq ft (86.50 m²)
Armament: nose 20-mm MG FF cannon, dorsal 13-mm (0.51-in) MG 131 gun, two ventral 7.2-mm (0.31-in) MG 15 guns, two beam 7.9-mm (0.31-in) MG 81 guns; 4,409 lb (2000 kg) bombs both internally and externally

Heinkel He 115

With forward-firing 20-mm MG 151 cannon, this late-series Heinkel He 115C-1 served with 1.Staffel, Kustenfliegergruppe 406. It carried five 7.7-mm (0.303-in) MG 15 and 17 machine-guns, and a fuel tank.

The large twin-float **Heinkel He 115** monoplane was first flown in prototype form in 1936, powered by two 960-hp (716-kW) BMW 132K radials. In 1938 production **He 115A-1**s joined the Luftwaffe as three-seat general-purpose duties aircraft armed with single 7.92-mm (0.31-in) guns in the nose and rear cockpit, followed by the **He 115A-3** with revised bomb bay and radio equipment. The **He 115B-1** with increased fuel capacity was delivered in 1939. The **He 115B-2** came soon after with load capability of one 2,205-lb (1000-kg) parachute mine and a 1,102-lb (500-kg) bomb load; it also featured strengthened floats which allowed operation from ice and snow. On these aircraft fell the task of minelaying in British waters during the first two years of the war, serving in particular with Kustenfliegergruppen 106, 506 and 906. The **He 115C** series introduced a modified nose mounting a single 20-mm MG 151 cannon. The **He 115C-2** had the reinforced floats of the **He 115B-2**, and was followed by the **He 115C-3** minelayer and the **He 115C-4** torpedo-bomber. He 115s of KuFlGr 406 were prominent in their attacks on the North Cape PQ convoys in 1942. Very few of the four-

crew **He 115D** series were produced. Production of the He 115 ceased in 1942 but – surprisingly, in view of Germany's heavy production priorities elsewhere – it restarted in 1943 with the **He 115E-1** multi-purpose aircraft, which was similar to the He 115C series but mounted twin 7.92-mm (0.31-in) guns in the nose and rear positions; some aircraft also featured the 20-mm MG 151 cannon. Total production of the He 115 was about 500 aircraft.

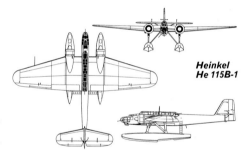

*Heinkel
He 115B-1*

Specification: Heinkel He 115B-1

Type: three-crew torpedo-bomber and minelayer

Powerplant: two 970-hp (724-kW) BMW 132K radial pistons

Performance: max speed 220 mph (355 km/h) at 11,155 ft (3400 m); climb rate 771 ft (235 m) per minute; ceiling 18,045 ft (5500 m); range 1,243 miles (2000 km)

Weights: empty 11,684 lb (5300 kg); max take-off 22,928 lb (10400 kg)

Dimensions: span 72 ft 2⅛ in (22.20 m); length 56 ft 9¼ in (17.30 m); height 21 ft 7⅞ in (6.60 m); wing area 933.3 sq ft (86.70 m²)

Armament: flexible 7.92-mm (0.31-in) MG 15 gun in nose and rear cockpit; one 1,764-lb (800-kg) torpedo or 2,205-lb (1000-kg) parachute mine; two 551-lb (250-kg) bombs

The Heinkel He 115 was one of the most efficient of all floatplanes used in Europe during the war. Early aircraft were employed mainly for minelaying and coastal reconnaissance; production was phased out in 1940 but reinstated in 1943-44.

Heinkel He 177 Greif

This He 177A-5 belonged to II. Gruppe, Kampfgeschwader 1 'Hindenburg' based at Prowenhren, East Prussia, in mid-1944. Led by Oberstleutnant Horst von Riesen, KG 1 assembled about 90 of these bombers for attacks on Russia.

In 1938 the RLM approached the Heinkel company with a requirement for a heavy bomber. The resultant four-engined mid-wing **He 177 Greif** (Griffon) had 1,000-hp (746-kW) DB 601 engines coupled in pairs (termed DB 606s) to drive single propellers. The first aircraft, the **He 177V1**, was flown on 19 November 1939. Continuing engine overheating problems and persistent structural failures delayed production, the first **He 177A-1**s not reaching I./KG 40 for operational trials until July 1942. In the course of these trials, He 177s took part in raids on the UK, but generally they proved disappointing in service. Several sub-variants of the **He 177A-3** were produced, including the **He 177A-3/R3** carrying three Hs 293 anti-shipping weapons, the **He 177A-3/R5** with 75-mm gun in the ventral gondola and the **He 177A-3/R7** torpedo-bomber. He 177A-3s were used by FKGr 2 to fly supply missions to German forces at Stalingrad in January 1943. The **He 177A-5** incorporated a stronger wing to carry heavier external loads, and a small number were converted to the *Zerstörer* role with 33 upward-firing rocket tubes in the normal bomb bays. Small numbers of He 177A-5s returned to

night attack on the UK early in 1944. This latter version was the last to serve with the Luftwaffe (bombers being afforded low priority during the last year of the war), but many interesting projects continued to be pursued, including the conversion of He 177V38 as a carrier of Germany's atomic bomb, which in the event did not materialise.

Heinkel He 177A-5/R6

The big Heinkel Greif bombers (He 177A-5 seen here), originally intended to provide the Luftwaffe with a strategic bombing force, encountered so many development problems that they only entered service in quantity during the last 18 months of the war. About 1,160 production and 30 prototype He 177s were built.

Specification: Heinkel He 177A-5/R2 Greif
Type: six-crew bomber
Powerplant: two 2,950-hp (2200-kW) Daimler-Benz DB 610A 1/B-1 inline pistons
Performance: max speed 303 mph (488 km/h) at 19,685 ft (6000 m); climb rate 623 ft (190 m) per minute; ceiling 26,245 ft (8000 m); range (with two Hs 293) 3,418 miles (5500 km)
Weights: empty 37,257 lb (16900 kg); max take-off 68,342 lb (31000 kg)
Dimensions: span 103 ft 1¾ in (31.44 m); length 66 ft 11¼ in (20.40 m); height 20 ft 11¾ in (6.40 m); wing area 1,098.0 sq ft (102.00 m²)
Armament: nose 7.92-mm (0.31-in) MG 81 gun, 13-mm (0.51-in) MG 131 gun in forward & rear dorsal turrets & ventral gondola, 20-mm MG FF cannon in ventral gondola & tail; max bomb load 13,228 lb (6000 kg) or two Hs 293 weapons

Heinkel He 219 Uhu

This Heinkel He 219A belonged to 1. Staffel, Nachtjagdgeschwader 1 based at Munster-Handorf in the autumn of 1944. 1./NJG 1 was the first unit to fly the He 219 in combat. The Roman IV on the nose identifies the radar as Lichtenstein SN-2.

Without doubt the best German night-fighter of the war, the **He 219 Uhu** (Owl) possessed in abundance all three attributes essential for such combat: high speed, heavy gun armament and efficient radar. The **He 219V1** was flown on 15 November 1942 and production examples would have followed quickly had an RAF raid on Rostock not destroyed more than three-quarters of the design drawings. Pre-production **He 219A-0**s were delivered to NJG 1 at Venlo in April 1943, and on the first combat sortie Major Werner Streib destroyed five Lancasters within 30 minutes on 11-12 June. The first version to be produced in quantity was the **He 219A-5** with two 30-mm and two 20-mm cannon. At the end of 1943 the He 219 was officially abandoned on the grounds that the Ju 88G was capable of catching the Lancaster and Halifax but, as the He 219 was the only night-fighter able to deal with the Mosquito, production continued. The major variant, the **He 219A-7**, was introduced in 1944. The **He 219A-7/R1** was armed with no fewer than eight cannon, four forward-firing 30-mm and two of 20-mm, plus two upward-firing 30-mm guns in a *schrage Musik* (slanting music, or

jazz) installation. Fastest of all the He 219A series versions was the **He 219A-7/R6** with 2,500-hp (1865-kW) Jumo 222A/B engines and a top speed of 435 mph (700 km/h). Most aircraft were equipped with FuG 220 Lichtenstein SN-2 radar. Of all RAF Mosquitoes lost during night operations more than 60 per cent (estimated) fell to He 219s.

Heinkel He 219A-5/R1

Specification: Heinkel He 219A-7/R1 Uhu
Type: two-seat high-altitude night-fighter
Powerplant: two 1,800-hp (1343-kW) Daimler-Benz DB 603E inline pistons
Performance: max speed 416 mph (670 km/h) at 22,965 ft (7000 m); climb rate 1,805 ft (550 m) per minute; ceiling 41,665 ft (12700 m); range 1,243 miles (2000 km)
Weights: empty 24,691 lb (11200 kg); loaded 33,730 lb (15300 kg)
Dimensions: span 60 ft 8½ in (18.50 m); length 50 ft 11¾ in (15.54 m); height 13 ft 5½ in (4.10 m); wing area 479.0 sq ft (44.50 m²)
Armament: two 30-mm MK 108 cannon in wingroots, two 30-mm MK 103 and two 20-mm MG 151/20 in ventral gun tray, two upward-firing 30-mm MK 108 cannon in rear cockpit

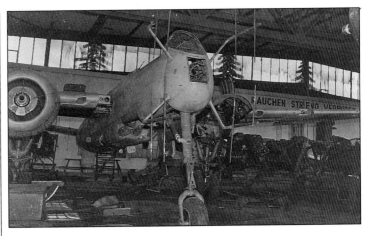

This He 219 is seen undergoing maintenance after being captured intact at Bindback, near Bayreuth, on a field taken by the 11th Armored Division of the US Third Army. Note the radar antenna on the aircraft's nose.

Henschel Hs 123

This Henschel Hs 123A-1 bears the markings of II.(Schlacht)/ Lehrgeschwader 2, a unit which – given specific cover by the Bf 109Es of I./JG 21 – took an active part in close support operations during the Battle of France in 1940.

The **Henschel Hs 123** single-seat ground-support biplane stemmed from one of the first requirements prepared for the new Luftwaffe in 1933. Of all-metal construction, the prototype Hs 123 was powered by the 650-hp (485-kW) BMW 132A-3 radial and first flew in the spring of 1935. Production **Hs 123A-1**s appeared in mid-1936 with 880-hp (656-kW) BMW 132Dc engines and were armed with two 7.92-mm (0.31-in) MG 17 guns in the nose; a single 551-lb (250-kg) bomb could be carried between the landing gear legs. They soon joined the Luftwaffe's first dive-bomber *Geschwader*, but when some aircraft were sent to fight in the Spanish Civil War they came to be employed as ground support aircraft. After the introduction of the Junkers Ju 87 it was in the latter role that the Hs 123 survived in Luftwaffe service. By the outbreak of war in September 1939, production was already being brought to an end and only II.(S)/LG 2 was still equipped with the aircraft. This unit continued to fly the old biplane in combat, participating in the Polish campaign and in the Blitzkrieg attack in the west of May 1940, and was still flying them during the invasion of the Balkans in April 1941.

During the early stages of the attack on the Soviet Union, some Hs 123s were armed with a pair of 20-mm cannon and were adapted to carry 92 4.4-lb (2-kg) anti-personnel bombs; so effective were they that suggestions were put forward for the aircraft to re-enter production, but the plan proved impractical. II.(S)/LG 2 (redesignated II./SG 2) retained the veteran biplanes until, in mid-1944, they were finally withdrawn from service.

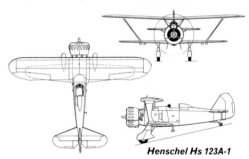

Henschel Hs 123A-1

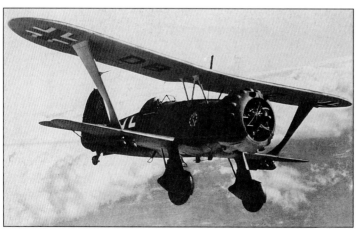

Like obsolete biplanes elsewhere (such as Britain's Gladiator and Italy's Fiat CR.42), the Henschel Hs 123 gave surprisingly good service well into the war. This Hs 123B wears the Sturmabzeichen (close combat medal insignia) and is carrying four 110-lb (50-kg) bombs under its wings.

Specification:
Henschel Hs 123A-1
Type: single-seat close support biplane
Powerplant: one 880-hp (656-kW) BMW 132Dc radial piston
Performance: max speed 212 mph (341 km/h) at 3,940 ft (1200 m); initial climb rate 2,953 ft (900 m) per minute; service ceiling 29,530 ft (9000 m); range 534 miles (860 km)
Weights: empty 3,307 lb (1500 kg); max take-off 4,883 lb (2215 kg)
Dimensions: span 34 ft 5½ in (10.50 m); length 27 ft 4 in (8.33 m); height 10 ft 6⅜ in (3.21 m); wing area 267.5 sq ft (24.86 m²)
Armament: two synchronised 7.92-mm (0.31-in) MG 17 machine-guns in nose; max 992 lb (450 kg) of bombs

Henschel Hs 126

Bearing the markings of 2.(H)/31, this Hs 126 has had its wheel spats removed for ease of operating from rough fields. The Hs 126 was a common sight over the advancing German armoured columns during the Battle of France in 1940.

Designed to meet much the same type of requirement as the Westland Lysander in British service, the **Henschel Hs 126** battlefield reconnaissance aircraft first flew in **Hs 126V1** form (a conversion of the Hs 122B-O) towards the end of 1936, the powerplant being a Junkers Jumo 210C inline. This aircraft was generally deemed unsuitable for service use, and was followed by the **Hs 126V2** and **Hs 126V3** prototypes with redesigned vertical tails and Bramo Fafnir 323 radial powerplant. Service tests followed with the generally similar **Hs 126A-0** series, of which 10 were built, before the 880-hp (656-kW) BMW 132Dc radial-powered **Hs 126A-1** entered service during late 1938 with Aufklarungsgruppe 35 in Germany and Aufklarungsstaffel 88 in Spain. By the outbreak of war in September 1939 the production version was the definitive **Hs 126B-1**, which was powered by the 900-hp (671-kW) Bramo 323A and had superior radio equipment. It was this model which played a prominent part in the Polish and French campaigns of 1939 and 1940, respectively, spotting and reconnoitring for the rapid-moving Panzer forces of the German army. By the time of the German invasion of Russia in June 1941, no fewer than 48 *Staffeln* were equipped with He 126B-1s. These played their part in the early days of the campaign, but soon had to be provided with fighter cover as Russian fighter strength grew, and had finally to be withdrawn from daylight operations. By 1944 they were restricted to nocturnal harassing raids with the *Nachtschlachtgruppen* over the Eastern Front. Production totalled about 800.

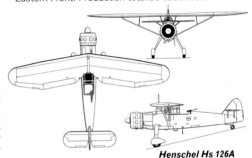

Henschel Hs 126A

Specification:
Henschel Hs 126B-1
Type: two-crew battlefield reconnaissance aircraft
Powerplant: one 900-hp (671-kW) Bramo 323A-2 radial piston
Performance: max speed 221 mph (356 km/h) at 9,845 ft (3000 m); climb to 13,125 ft (4000 m) in 7.2 minutes; ceiling 27,000 ft (8230 m); range 360 miles (560 km)
Weights: empty 4,475 lb (2030 kg); max take-off 7,209 lb (3270 kg)
Dimensions: span 47 ft 6¾ in (14.50 m); length 35 ft 7 in (10.84 m); height 12 ft 3½ in (3.74 m); wing area 340.14 sq ft (31.60 m²)
Armament: one forward-firing 7.92-mm (0.31-in) MG 17 machine-gun, one flexible 7.92-mm (0.31-in) MG 15 machine-gun in rear cockpit; max 331 lb (150 kg) of bombs

Vital but least spectacular component of the Blitzkrieg concept, the Henschel Hs 126 undertook battlefield surveillance, spotting for artillery and providing short-range photo-reconnaissance. It was flown in almost every German campaign until replaced by the Fw 189 from 1942.

Henschel Hs 129

This Henschel Hs 129B-1 belonged to 8./Schlachtgeschwader 1, which formed at Lippstadt and was operational over Kursk Salient in the summer of 1943. In October the unit was redesignated 11.(Pz)/SG 9.

The single-seat ground-support **Henschel Hs 129** was the outcome of an imaginative – if speculative – requirement in 1937 for a heavily armoured twin-engined aircraft to perform an anti-tank role. Designed by Friedrich Nicolaus, the **Hs 129V1** prototype was first flown in 1938 with two 465-hp (347-kW) Argus As 410 inline engines; it proved to be underpowered, cramped for the pilot and sluggish on the controls. These severe criticisms resulted in re-engining some of the pre-production **Hs 129A-0**s with captured French 700-hp (522-kW) Gnome-Rhône 14M radials. Development **Hs 129B-0**s with these engines, increased cockpit space and electrically operated trim tabs were delivered in December 1941, followed by production **Hs 129B-1**s in 1942. The majority of Hs 129s served with units on the Eastern Front, playing an outstanding part in destroying Russian armour in the great battle of Kursk of July 1943, but also in North Africa where they met with less success. A large number of armament variations were developed, including the **Hs 129B-1/R2** with a 30-mm MK 101 cannon under the nose with 30 rounds, the **Hs 129B-3** with a 75-mm BK 7,5 anti-tank gun

with 12 rounds, and numerous *Rüstsatz* variations combining light anti-personnel and fragmentation bombs with 7.92-mm (0.31-in), 13-mm (0.51-in), 15-mm (0.59-in), 20-mm and 30-mm guns. They could wreak considerable damage among Russian armoured vehicles, the 75-mm gun proving capable of penetrating the armour of KV-1 and T-34 tanks.

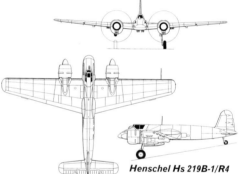

Henschel Hs 219B-1/R4

An Hs 129B-2/R2 of 4./Schlachtgeschwader 1 is seen on the Eastern Front in the summer of 1943. The aircraft eventually proved fairly successful for ground attack, being heavily armed and armoured, although the engines were somewhat underpowered and unreliable. A total of 858 Hs 129s was built from 1942-1944.

Specification: Henschel Hs 129B-1/R2
Type: single-seat anti-tank ground-support aircraft
Powerplant: two 700-hp (522-kW) Gnome-Rhône 14M radial pistons
Performance: max speed 253 mph (407 km/h) at 12,750 ft (3830 m); time to 9,845 ft (3000 m) 7.0 minutes; service ceiling 29,530 ft (9000 m); range 348 miles (560 km)
Weights: empty 8,783 lb (3984 kg); max take-off 11,263 lb (5109 kg)
Dimensions: span 46 ft 7 in (14.20 m); length 31 ft 11¾ in (9.75 m); height 10 ft 8 in (3.25 m); wing area 312.16 sq ft (29.00 m²)
Armament: two 20-mm MG 151/20 and two 7.92-mm (0.31-in) MG 17 guns in nose, one 30-mm MK 101 cannon with 30 rounds under nose; bomb load 772 lb (350 kg)

Ilyushin Il-2

This Il-2m3 lacks its rear cockpit canopy, which was often removed in the field to afford the rear gunner better visibility and field of fire. The lines inscribed on the fuselage forward of the wind screen helped in judging gravity drop when firing air-to-ground rockets.

Widely referred to as the 'Stormovik' (although the Russian *Shturmovik* applied to all ground attack aircraft), Sergei Ilyushin's rugged **Il-2** was feared by the German soldier on the Eastern Front as the *Schwarz Tod* (Black Death). The first prototype, a single-seater known as the **TsKB-57**, made its maiden flight late in 1939 flown by V. Kokkinaki. With a heavily armoured front fuselage and later powered by a 1,680-hp (1253-kW) AM-38 inline engine, the prototype underwent state trials in March 1941 and entered production as the Il-2, 249 aircraft being completed before the German attack of June that year. Early experience showed the necessity of providing a gunner for rear defence and, with a lengthened armoured 'bath', the **Il-2m3** two-seater appeared in August 1942. An improved version, the **Il-2m3(mod)**, was introduced soon afterwards with the 23-mm VYa cannon in the wings replaced by 37-mm Il-P-37 guns. This version fought during the great tank battles around Kursk in July 1943, proving capable of destroying the German Pzkpfw VI Tiger tank; they were later armed with RS-132 13.2-cm (5.2-in) rockets with hollow-charge warheads. Some Il-2m3(mod)s of

Soviet naval aviation (**Il-2T**) carried fittings for a single 53.3 cm (21-in) torpedo, while a trainer version, the **Il-2U**, was also produced in naval aviation workshops. Some sources put the number produced at over 35,000, although this most likely included some aircraft with the 2,000-hp (1492-kW) AM-42 engine that was later designated **Il-10**.

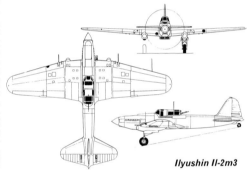

Ilyushin Il-2m3

Specification: Ilyushin Il-2m3(mod)

Type: two-seat ground-attack aircraft

Powerplant: one 1,770-hp (1320-kW) AM-38F inline piston

Performance: max speed 251 mph (404 km/h) at 4,920 ft (1500 m); service ceiling 19,685 ft (6000 m); range 373 miles (600 km)

Weights: empty 9,590 lb (4350 kg); max take-off 14,021 lb (6360 kg)

Dimensions: span 48 ft 0½ in (14.60 m); length 38 ft 0½ in (11.60 m); height 11 ft 1½ in (3.40 m); wing area 414.4 sq ft (38.50 m²)

Armament: two forward-firing 23-mm VYa cannon, two 7.62-mm (0.3-in) ShKAS machine-guns, one 12.7-mm (0.5-in) UBT machine-gun in rear cockpit; bomb load 1,321 lb (600 kg) or rocket projectiles

The importance attached by the Russians to the Il-2 may be judged by the terms of a telegram from Stalin to a factory that had fallen behind with deliveries: "The Red Army needs the Il-2 as it needs air or bread. I demand more. This is my last warning." Large numbers of Il-2s were destroyed by flak and German fighters.

Ilyushin Il-4

Used by both the Soviet air force and navy, the Il-4 was a rugged medium bomber of which more than 10,000 were produced between 1940 and 1944. During the latter part of this period the aircraft were built with many wooden components.

The prototype of this low-wing twin-engined bomber, designated **TsKB-26**, flew in 1935 and was developed through the **TsKB-30**. It entered production in 1937 as the **DB-3** (DB is a Russian contraction denoting long-range bomber). Early examples were powered by 765-hp (571-kW) M-85 engines, but these were replaced by 960-hp (716-kW) M-86s in 1938. Although a tough and simple design, the aircraft suffered from a poor defensive armament of single nose, dorsal and ventral 7.62-mm (0.3-in) guns, and lost heavily to such aircraft as the Bulldog, Gladiator and Fokker D.XXI during the Winter War against Finland in 1939-40. In 1939 a modified version with lengthened nose (the **DB-3F**) appeared and, in 1940, in conformity with changed Russian practice, the designation became **Il-4** (denoting the designer, Sergei Ilyushin). Soon after the German attack on Russia opened in 1941 Il-4 production was withdrawn to plants in Siberia, and a large proportion of the metal structure was replaced by less strategically critical wood. Il-4s also entered service with Soviet naval aviation, and it was a naval-manned force of these bombers that first raided Berlin from the east on 8 August 1941.

Thereafter the Il-4 paid frequent visits to the German capital and other targets in Eastern Europe. In 1944 production ended, although the Il-4 served until the end of the war and afterwards. Apart from increasing the calibre of its guns and giving it a torpedo-carrying ability, the Il-4 remained virtually unchanged between 1941 and 1944.

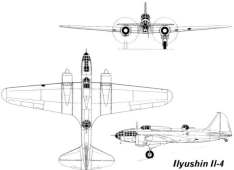

Ilyushin Il-4

As well as being employed as a bomber (it raided Berlin many times), the Il-4 was flown as a reconnaissance aircraft and glider tug. It was characterised by poor defensive armament and suffered fairly heavy losses, particularly to German night-fighters on the Eastern Front.

Specification: Ilyushin Il-4
Type: four-crew bomber/torpedo-bomber
Powerplant: two 1,100-hp (821-kW) M-88B radial pistons
Performance: max speed 255 mph (411 km/h) at 15,500 ft (4725 m); climb rate 886 ft (270 m) per minute; ceiling 32,810 ft (10000 m); range with bomb load 1,616 miles (2600 km)
Weights: empty 13,228 lb (6000 kg); max take-off 22,046 lb (10000 kg)
Dimensions: span 70 ft 4¼ in (21.44 m); length 48 ft 6½ in (14.80 m); height 13 ft 5½ in (4.10 m); wing area 718.0 sq ft (66.7 m²)
Armament: 12.7-mm (0.5-in) UBT machine-gun in nose, dorsal turret and ventral positions; max bomb load 2,205 lb (1000 kg) or three 1,102-lb (500-kg) torpedoes

Junkers Ju 52/3m

This Junkers Ju 52/3mg7e is from Stab IV/Transportgeschwader 1 on the Courland Front, seen in the winter of 1944-45. Versions of the Ju 52 were the major transport aircraft for the Luftwaffe in all theatres throughout the war.

Affectionately known throughout the German forces as *Tante Ju* (Auntie Junkers), the three-engined **Ju 52/3m** with characteristic corrugated metal skin was widely used as a pre-war commercial airliner before being employed, first as a bomber and later as a troop transport, by the Luftwaffe. The **Ju 52/3mg3e** was flown in both roles by the Legion Condor in Spain from 1936. On the eve of the invasion of Poland, the Luftwaffe fielded 552 transports, of which no fewer than 547 were Ju 52/3ms (the **Ju 52/3mg4e** and **Ju 52/3mg5e** versions, these aircraft featuring provision for alternative wheel, float or ski landing gear). Improved radio identified the **Ju 52/3mg6e**, and one of the main production versions, the **Ju 52/3mg7e**, featured automatic pilot, wider loading doors and accommodation for 18 assault troops. The **Ju 52/3mg8e** introduced increased cabin windows and a 13-mm (0.51-in) machine-gun in a dorsal position, and the **Ju 52/3mg9e** glider tug was stressed for increased take-off weight. The **Ju 52/3mg10e** was powered by BMW 132L radials. The final version, introduced late in 1943 when Allied fighters posed a greatly increased threat in all theatres, featured a 7.92-mm (0.31-in) gun over the cockpit. Famous battles and campaigns in which the sturdy old workhorse participated included Norway, Crete, Demyansk (where some 200 Ju 52/3ms airlifted 24,000 tons of relief supplies, 15,000 troops and 20,000 casualties in three months), Stalingrad and Tunisia.

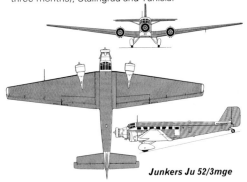

Junkers Ju 52/3mge

Constantly derided by Allied observers on account of its austere appearance and corrugated metal skinning, the Junkers Ju 52/3m proved robust and reliable in Luftwaffe service. More important, it was readily available. Estimates of total Ju 52/3m production (in Germany and elsewhere) vary from 5,600 to 5,900.

Junkers Ju 87

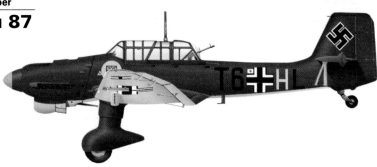

This Junkers Ju 87B-2 belonged to 3./Stukageschwader 2 'Immelmann' and is seen as it would have appeared during the Battle of Britain. This aircraft crash-landed at Selsey in August 1940, following a raid on RAF Tangmere.

Forever deprecated as a Nazi terror weapon, the **Junkers Ju 87** (referred to as the 'Stuka', a contraction of the word *Sturzkampfflugzeug*) was an imaginative weapon of considerable accuracy when operating in skies clear of enemy fighters. Conceived as a form of support artillery for the Wehrmacht's *Blitzkrieg* tactics, the Ju 87 was first flown in 1935, a small number of **Ju 87A-1**s and **Ju 87B-1**s flying in Spain in 1938-39. To support the invasion of Poland, the Luftwaffe fielded all five *Stukageschwader* by then equipped with Ju 87s, and it was in this campaign that, with little effective opposition in the air, the legend of the 'Stuka' was born. With sirens screaming, the cranked-wing dive-bombers effectively destroyed the country's lines of communication, bridges, railways and airfields. During the difficult Norwegian campaign the **Ju 87R** with underwing fuel tanks was introduced to cope with the great distances involved, and in the Battle of Britain this version and the **Ju 87B** were heavily committed until withdrawn temporarily due to losses. At the end of 1941 the **Ju 87D**, a much cleaned-up version with Jumo 211 engine, entered service on the Russian Front, and appeared in North Africa the following year. The **Ju 87G**, a specialist anti-tank aircraft, featured a pair of 37-mm guns under the wings and achieved much success. The greatest exponent of the 'Stuka' was Hans-Ulrich Rudel, whose personal tally of a battleship, a cruiser and a destroyer sunk, and 519 tanks destroyed, far exceeded any other.

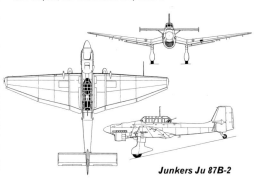

Junkers Ju 87B-2

This Ju 87D belonged to Stukageschwader 2. In the absence of opposing fighters, tight formations of Ju 87s could deliver devastating tactical firepower, paving the way for tanks and infantry. Total Ju 87 production was said to be 5,709.

Specification: Junkers Ju 87D-7
Type: two-seat dive-bomber
Powerplant: one 1,500-hp (1119-kW) Junkers Jumo 211P inline piston
Performance: max speed 248 mph (400 km/h) at 15,750 ft (4800 m); service ceiling 27,885 ft (8500 m); range 410 miles (660 km)
Weights: empty 8,686 lb (3940 kg); max take-off 14,550 lb (6600 kg)
Dimensions: span 49 ft 2½ in (15.00 m); length 37 ft 8¾ in (11.50 m); height 12 ft 9½ in (3.90 m); wing area 362.7 sq ft (33.60 m²)
Armament: two forward-firing 20-mm MG 151/20 cannon, two 7.92-mm (0.31-in) MG 81 guns in rear cockpit; bomb load one 3,968-lb (1800-kg) bomb under fuselage, two 1,102-lb (500-kg) bombs under wings

Junkers Ju 88

This Ju 88A-5 belonged to III./Lehrgeschwader 1, based at Catania for operations by X Fliegerkorps against Malta. The Ju 88A-5's strong landing gear made it suitable for Sicilian airfields.

The **Ju-88** was used as a low-, medium- and high-level bomber, night-fighter and intruder, torpedo-bomber, anti-tank fighter and pilotless missile. The prototype **Ju 88V1** flew on 21 December 1936 and, by the end of 1939, 60 **Ju 88A-1s** had been completed. The **Ju 88A-4** entered service in 1940 with increased span and armament, while the first **Ju 88C** *Zerstörer* had already seen combat in the Battle of Britain. The **Ju 88C-6b** night-fighter was introduced in 1942 with Lichtenstein airborne radar, and from this stemmed the **Ju 88R** with BMW 801 engines in place of the customary Jumo 211s, and the **Ju 88G**, similarly powered and with revised tail and increased armament. Development of the Ju 88A led to the **Ju 88A-4 Trop** being employed in North Africa, the **Ju 88A-6/U** as a three-seat maritime bomber with search radar, the **Ju 88A-7** and **Ju 88A-12** as dual-control trainers, the **Ju 88A-13** as a heavily-armoured ground attack bomber, and the **Ju 88A-17** as an anti-shipping strike aircraft capable of carrying two torpedoes. The **Ju 88D** was powered by Jumo 211D engines, and the **Ju 88P** was a specialist ground-attack version with the 'solid' nose of the Ju 88C and a variety of heavy guns, including 75-mm, 50-mm and 37-mm cannon; there were even plans to fit an 88-mm Duka gun, and a flame-thrower. The high-altitude **Ju 88S** fast bomber was powered by nitrous oxide-boosted BMW 801Gs, and the **Ju 88H** and **Ju 88T** were photo-reconnaissance series.

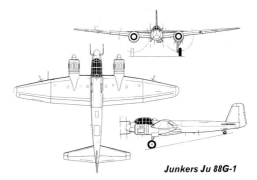

Junkers Ju 88G-1

Specification: Junkers Ju 88A-4
Type: four-crew bomber
Powerplant: two 1,340-hp (1000-kW) Junkers Jumo 211J-2 inline pistons
Performance: max speed 292 mph (470 km/h) at 17,390 ft (5300 m); climb to 17,715 ft (5400 m) in 23 minutes; service ceiling 26,900 ft (8200 m); range 1,106 miles (1780 km)
Weights: empty 21,737 lb (9860 kg); max take-off 30,864 lb (14000 kg)
Dimensions: span 65 ft 7½ in (20.00 m); length 47 ft 2¾ in (14.40 m); height 15 ft 11 in (4.85 m); wing area 586.7 sq ft (54.50 m²)
Armament: two 7.92-mm (0.31-in) MG 81 guns firing forward and two in dorsal position; two ventral 7.62-mm (0.31-in) MG 81s; max bomb load (internal and external) 6,614 lb (3000 kg)

This aircraft is the prototype V1 of the Ju 88G medium bomber. The Ju 88 soon proved itself a magnificently versatile aircraft, with a structure able to absorb massive combat damage and widely differing combat loads. Production of the Ju 88 totalled at least 14,980.

Junkers Ju 188

This reconnaissance Ju 188D-2 is from 1. Staffel, Fernaufklarungsgruppe 124, based at Kirkenes, Norway. Equipped with FuG 200 search radar, these aircraft provided information on North Cape convoys for attacks by torpedo-bombers.

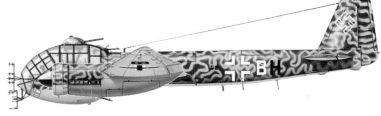

Delays with a radical Ju 288 development of the Ju 88 prompted the German air ministry to pursue an interim version – the **Ju 188** – late in 1942, pre-production **Ju 188B-0**s being completed in February 1943. Powered by 1,600-hp (1194-kW) BMW 801 radials, the new version featured the revised tail unit of the Ju 88G and, apart from sharply pointed wingtips, was a generally cleaned-up version of the older aircraft, although early versions produced little improvement in load-carrying and performance. First operations by the Ju 188 over the UK were in August 1943, and soon afterwards the aircraft were employed as pathfinders. Produced in parallel was the photo-reconnaissance **Ju 188F** series with 1,700-hp (1268-kW) BMW 801Ds. The **Ju 188A-1**, with water methanol-boosted 2,240-hp (1671-kW) Jumo 213A-1 engines, did not appear until January 1944, the **Ju 188A-3** being a torpedo-bomber sub-variant. The **Ju 188D** was a photo-reconnaissance version of the Ju 188A. The **Ju 188E-2** was a torpedo bomber. By then, Germany's priorities were weighted in favour of fighter production and the Ju 188 was terminated in the spring of 1944 after 1,076 had been completed. Photo-reconnaissance versions continued in service until the end of the war. The fastest version was the **Ju 188T** which, with three-speed two-stage supercharged and nitrous oxide-boosted 2,168-hp (1617-kW) Jumo 213E-1 engines, achieved 435 mph (700 km/h).

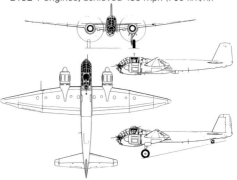

Junkers Ju 188E-1 (upper view: Ju 188E-2)

This aircraft is an example of the E version of the Ju 188. The Ju 188 was one of the principal bombers used by the Luftwaffe during Operation Steinbock, the resumption of air attacks on London in 1944.

Specification: Junkers Ju 188E-1
Type: five-crew bomber
Powerplant: two 1,600-hp (1194-kW) BMW 801ML radial pistons
Performance: max speed 311 mph (500 km/h) at 19,685 ft (6000 m); climb to 19,685 ft (6000 m) in 17.6 minutes; ceiling 31,510 ft (9300 m); range 1,211 miles (195 km)
Weights: empty 2,737 lb (9860 kg); loaded 31,989 lb (14510 kg)
Dimensions: span 72 ft 2 in (22.00 m); length 49 ft 0½ in (14.95 m); height 14 ft 6 ¾ in (4.44 m); wing area 602.8 sq ft (56.00 m²)
Armament: 20-mm MG 151/20 cannon in nose and dorsal turret, 13-mm (0.51-in) MG 131 machine-gun in rear dorsal and rear ventral positions; max bomb load 6,614 lb (3000 kg)

Kawanishi H6K 'Mavis'

The graceful Kawanishi H6K long-range maritime patrol aircraft was one of the best Japanese operational aircraft when the Pacific war started. Later versions had a range of 4,208 miles (6772 km).

The **H6K** maritime reconnaissance flying-boat owed some of its design to the work of Short Bros in the early 1930s, although its parasol wing layout was more akin to contemporary American designs. Powered by four 840-hp (627-kW) Nakajima Hikari 2 radials, the first of four **H6K1** prototypes flew on 14 July 1936. Production **H6K2**s followed in 1939 with 1,000-hp (746-kW) Mitsubishi Kinsei 43 radials, together with a staff transport version, the **H6K3**. The principal production aircraft was the **H6K4**, of which a total of 127 was produced between 1939 and 1942. This version featured considerably increased fuel capacity, which bestowed a maximum range of 3,780 miles (6083 km), compared, for example, with 2,350 miles (3782 km) for the American PBY-5A Catalina. At the time of the attack on Pearl Harbor Japan's navy possessed 64 H6K4s, some of which were employed as long-range bombers for attacks on the East Indies; however, as Allied fighter opposition improved the aircraft returned to the maritime reconnaissance role, a task for which they were well suited over the vast distances of the Pacific. A new version appeared in 1942 – the **H6K5** – with more powerful engines and further increased fuel capacity, 36 examples being produced. A number of transports, the **H6K2-L** and **H6K4-L** versions, were also produced, bringing the total production of the H6K to 211, excluding prototypes.

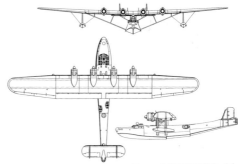

Kawanishi H6K5 'Mavis'

Specification:
Kawanishi H6K5
Type: nine-crew maritime reconnaissance flying-boat
Powerplant: four 1,300-hp (970-kW) Mitsubishi Kinsei 53 radial pistons
Performance: max speed 239 mph (385 km/h) at 19,685 ft (6000 m); climb to 16,405 ft (5000 m) in 13.38 minutes; ceiling 31,365 ft (9560 m); range 4,208 miles (6772 km)
Weights: empty 27,117 lb (12380 kg); max take-off 50,706 lb (23000 kg)
Dimensions: span 131 ft 2¾ in (40.00 m); length 84 ft 0⅛ in (25.63 m); height 20 ft 6¼ in (6.27 m); wing area 1,829.9 sq ft (170.00 m²)
Armament: 7.7-mm (0.303-in) Type 92 gun in bow turret, open dorsal position and each beam blister; one 20-mm Type 99 cannon in tail; bomb load 2,205 lb (1000 kg) or two 1,764-lb (800-kg) torpedoes

A total of 215 H6K flying-boats was produced between 1936 and 1943. The type was later used as a transport as well as occasionally for torpedo-bombing, as it was capable of carrying two torpedoes under the wing struts. The Allied names were 'Mavis' for the maritime reconnaissance versions, and 'Tillie' for the transports.

Kawanishi N1K 'George'

This Kawanishi N1K2-J was from the 343rd Kokutai. It was Warrant Officer Kinsuke Muot of this unit who, single-handedly, engaged 12 US Navy Hellcats in February 1945, shooting down four and forcing the others to break off combat.

In 1941 Kawanishi was still engaged in the design of the floatplane **N1K1**, intended as a naval fighter to support an island-hopping conquest in the Pacific without dependence on carriers or shore bases; in due course, 98 were produced (Allied name **'Rex'**). However, while their design was still in progress Kawanishi undertook a wheeled landing gear version, designated the **N1K1-J Shiden** (Violet Lightning). The prototype of the new fighter was flown on 27 December 1942, powered by the 18-cylinder Nakajima Homare radial. Production got under way in 1943 of the N1K1-J with a Homare 21 radial and an armament of two 7.7-mm (0.303-in) nose guns and four 20-mm wing cannon (two of which were carried in underwing fairings). Despite being plagued by constant engine troubles and an inherently weak landing gear, the Shiden was an excellent aircraft in combat, proving an equal match for the American F6F Hellcat and widely considered to be one of Japan's best wartime fighters. Three other main production versions were produced: the **N1K1-Ja** with nose guns deleted and all cannon mounted inside the wings; the **N1K1-Jb** with underwing racks for two 250-kg

(551-lb) bombs; and the **N1K1-Jc** with racks for four 250-kg (551-lb) bombs. A new version, the **N1K2-J**, with improved landing gear, redesigned vertical tail surfaces and cleaner engine cowling, appeared during the last year of the war and proved even better than the N1K1.

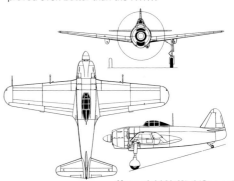

Kawanishi N1K2-J 'George'

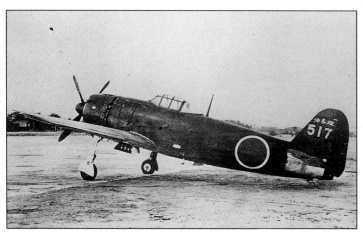

The N1K2-J proved to be one of the best Japanese bomber-destroyers, being armed with four 20-mm cannon in the wings but, like so many of that nation's best aircraft, there were too few of them too late. A total of 1,435 N1K Shidens was produced, with the Allied reporting name 'George'.

Specification:
Kawanishi N1K1-J 'George'
Type: single-seat fighter
Powerplant: one 1,990-hp (1485-kW) Nakajima NK9H Homare 21 radial piston
Performance: max speed 363 mph (584 km/h) at 19,355 ft (5900 m); climb to 19,685 ft (6000 m) in 7.8 minutes; service ceiling 41,010 ft (12500 m); range 890 miles (1432 km)
Weights: empty 6,387 lb (2897 kg); max take-off 9,526 lb (4321 kg)
Dimensions: span 39 ft 4¼ in (12.00 m); length 29 ft 1¾ in (8.89 m); height 13 ft 3⅛ in (4.06 m); wing area 252.95 sq ft (23.50 m²)
Armament: two 7.7-mm (0.303-in) Type 97 machine-guns in nose and four wing-mounted 20-mm Type 99 cannon

Kawasaki Ki-45 'Nick'

Ki-45s were widely used in defence against the American B-29 raids, claiming eight of the bombers on their first sortie. Production totalled 14 prototypes, 12 pre-production and 1,675 production aircraft.

Emulating the German heavy fighter (*Zerstörer*) concept, the Japanese issued a requirement in 1937 to which the Nakajima Ki-37, Kawasaki Ki-38 and Mitsubishi Ki-39 were submitted. The army seemed unable to agree specification priorities, but eventually Kawasaki was instructed to start work on a development of the Ki-38, the **Ki-45**. A twin Bristol Mercury-powered prototype was flown in January 1939, but subsequent development aircraft had 1,000-hp (746-kW) Nakajima Ha-25 radials. The designer, Takeo Doi, was working on a modified design to facilitate production, and in May 1941 the first **Ki-45 Kai** was completed, this being identifiable mainly by its straight-tapered wings and fin, and smooth-cowled engines. Named **Toryu** (Dragon Killer), the Ki-45 Kai entered service in August 1942 in China, and was first flown in action in Burma by the 16th Sentai during October. Popular due to its heavy armour protection and armament, it was a fairly fast aircraft and was used to intercept USAAF B-24 bombers (of the US 5th Air Force) and to attack ground targets, being capable of carrying two 250-kg (551 lb) bombs. One of the best night-fighters available to Japan, the **Ki-45**

KAIc, was introduced in 1944 with a semi-automatic 37-mm cannon in a ventral tunnel and two upward-firing 20-mm cannon; 477 of these aircraft were produced, but a radar-equipped version failed to reach service. A total of 1,701 of all versions of the 'Nick' was produced.

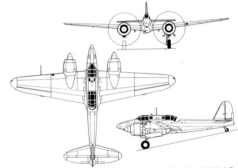

Kawasaki Ki-45 (Kai-hei 'Nick')

Versions of the Kawasaki Toryu included the Ki-45 KAIa heavy fighter, and the anti-shipping Ki-45 KAId. The Ki-45 KAIb derivative was dedicated to the ground attack and anti-ship roles, and had a revised armament of 37- or 75-mm cannon.

Kawasaki Ki-61 'Tony'

By the end of the war 13 Sentais were flying the Ki-61, the majority in defence of the Japanese homeland. Excluding prototypes and development aircraft, production totalled 1,380 Ki-61-Is, 1,274 Ki-61-I Kais and 374 Ki-61-IIs.

Sometimes described as a cross between a Messerschmitt Bf 109 and a P-51 Mustang, the **Kawasaki Ki-61** had the distinctive nose shape associated with an inverted-Vee inline engine; its Kawasaki Ha-40 was in effect a licence-built Daimler-Benz DB 601A. In December 1940 the designers were instructed to proceed with the Ki-61, and one year later the prototype was flown. The first production **Ki-61-1**s were deployed operationally in April 1943 when the 68th and 78th Sentais arrived in New Guinea. Named **Hien** (Swallow) in service (and codenamed **'Tony'** by the Allies), the new aircraft proved popular, being unusually well armed and armoured, and the type was at least a match for opposing American fighters. Its armament (of four 12.7-mm/0.5-in machineguns) proved inadequate to knock down enemy bombers, and the **Ki-61-I KAIc** was introduced with a pair of 20-mm cannon in the nose, these being replaced in a small number of **Ki-61-I KAId** fighters by two 30-mm cannon. The Ki-61-I and **Ki-61-I Kai** remained in production until 1945, but in 1944 they were joined in service by the **Ki-61-II**. with a more powerful Kawasaki Ha-140 inline (pro-

ducing 1,500 hp/1120 kW). With a top speed of 379 mph (610 km/h) this would have been an excellent fighter but for constant engine problems, and, when fully serviceable, the Ki-61-II was the only Japanese fighter fully able to combat the B-29 at its normal operating altitude, particularly when armed with four 20-mm cannon.

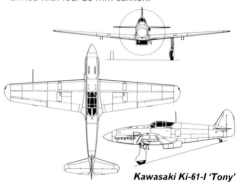

Kawasaki Ki-61-I 'Tony'

The Hien was Japan's only major fighter of World War II that incorporated an inline engine, and all variants of this fast and agile aircraft were plagued by engine problems. A version of the 'Tony' that was to have followed the Ki-61-II was the Ki-61-III, featuring a cut-down rear fuselage and 360° vision canopy.

Specification:
Kawasaki Ki-61-I KAIc 'Tony'
Type: single-seat fighter
Powerplant: one 1,180-hp (880-kW) Kawasaki Ha-40 inline piston
Performance: max speed 366 mph (590 km/h) at 13,980 ft (4260 m); climb to 16,405 ft (5000 m) in 7.0 minutes: service ceiling 32,810 ft (1000 m); range 1,120 miles (1800 km)
Weights: empty 5,798 lb (2630 kg); normal loaded 7,650 lb (3470 kg)
Dimensions: span 39 ft 4½ in (12.00 m); length 29 ft 4 in (8.94 m); height 12 ft 1¾ in (3.70 m); wing area 215.3 sq ft (20.00 m²)
Armament: two 20-mm Ho-5 cannon in nose and two 12.7-mm (0.5-in) Type 1 machine-guns in wings

Lavochkin LaGG-3

Designed by a committee headed by Semyon Lavochkin and including V. Gorbunov and M. Gudkov, the **LaGG-3** stemmed from the LaGG-1, whose prototype (the I-22) was first flown on 30 March 1939. These aircraft were unusual in retaining an all-wood structure; only the control surfaces, and later the landing flaps, were metal. This excellent little fighter was ordered into production in 1940 as the LaGG-1 with a 1,050-hp (783-kW) Klimov M-105 inline engine, but was too late to see service during the Winter War with Finland in 1939-40. With a top speed of 373 mph (600 km/h) and an armament of one 20-mm and two 12.7-mm (0.5-in) guns, the LaGG-1 was certainly one of the world's best fighters early in 1941. Pilots complained of poor climb performance and heavy controls, and a new version, the LaGG-3, was introduced by way of the **I-301** prototype after several hundred LaGG-1s had been delivered. At the time of the German attack, two air regiments still flew the older aircraft, but within a year four regiments had received the LaGG-3. Their task was to provide escort for the Il-2 close support aircraft, for which they carried a variety of armament combinations, including wing attachments for six 8.2-cm (3.23-in) rockets or light bombs. The LaGG-3 had a constant-speed propeller and improved rudder balancing, and was popular in service. Difficulties arose with field maintenance of the liquid-cooled M-105PFs, leading the Russians to opt for radial engines.

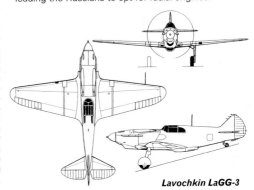

Lavochkin LaGG-3

This LaGG-3 was flown by Guards Captain Igor A. Katerov, 3 Guards IAP (Baltic Fleet) in the Lake Ladoga region in the winter of 1943-44. The type was robust and capable of sustaining considerable battle damage. Production ceased in 1942 with 1,200 built, preference being given to the radial-engined La-5 and La-7.

Lavochkin La-5/-7

This Lavochkin La-7 is from the Soviet 18th Guards Fighter Regiment. Essentially a low-altitude fighter, the Lavochkins were ideal as escorts for the slower and vulnerable Il-2 ground support aircraft.

As the Soviet armies reeled after the assault by Germany during 1941, frantic demands were made for modern equipment. Lavochkin started work on the LaG-5 fighter with 1,600-hp (1194-kW) M-82 radial, passing on almost immediately to a development, the **La-5**, with a cut-down rear fuselage which gave improved visibility. The prototype completed its acceptance trials in May 1942 and entered production two months later; by the end of the year 1,182 had been completed. In March 1943 the next and principal version, the **La-5FN**, entered production, a total of 21,975 aircraft, including the later **La-7**, being produced before the end of the war. The La-5FN featured the 1,650-hp (1231-kW) M-82FN engine, and its two 20-mm cannon were supplemented by four 82-mm RS 82 rocket projectiles or two PTAB anti-tank weapons. A two-seat trainer version, the **La-5UTI**, was also produced. Later aircraft had two 23-mm guns in place of the 20-mm weapons. In 1944 the La-7 appeared with an armament of three 20- or 23-mm cannon, an M-82FNU or FNV engine and a top speed of 423 mph (680 km/h). First large-scale use of the La-5 was at Stalingrad in November 1942. The aircraft

was a low/medium-altitude fighter, and during the great armour battles at Kursk in July 1943 La-5s were used as tank-busters. The highest-scoring Allied fighter pilot, Ivan Kojedub, achieved all his 62 combat victories in LaG-5s, La-5FNs and La-7s between 26 March 1943 and 19 April 1945.

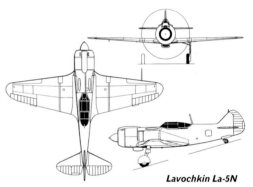

Lavochkin La-5N

In late 1941 Lavochkin re-engined an LaGG-3 with an ASh-82a radial, and when first flown in 1942 this aircraft was 25 mph (40 km/h) faster than the German Bf 109F at low level. The type – the La-5 – completely fulfilled the Soviets' requirement for a fast-climbing but highly manoeuvrable low-level interceptor.

Specification:
Lavochkin La-5FN
Type: single-seat fighter/fighter-bomber
Powerplant: one 1,650-hp (1231-kW) M-82FN radial piston
Performance: max speed 402 mph (647 km/h) at 16,405 ft (5000 m); climb to 3,280 ft (1000 m) in 0.35 minutes; service ceiling 32,810 ft (10000 m); range 435 miles (700 km)
Weights: empty 6,173 lb (2800 kg); normal loaded 7,408 lb (3360 kg)
Dimensions: span 32 ft 5¾ in (9.90 m); length 27 ft 10¾ in (8.50m); height 8 ft 4 in (2.54 m); wing area 201.8 sq ft (18.75 m²)
Armament: two nose-mounted 20-mm ShVAK cannon (on later aircraft 23-mm NS cannon); four 82-mm (3.23 in) RS 82 rockets or 331 lb (150 kg) of bombs

Lioré et Olivier LeO 451

*Lioré et Olivier 451 no.
426 belonged to the
1ere Escadrille, Groupe
de Bombardement I/II.
based at Orn-La Senia,
Morocco, in mid-1941.
This unit had suffered
heavy losses among its
LeO 45s during the
Battle of France before
moving to North Africa.*

After the French air force became independent on 1 April 1933, a number of 'Plans' were conceived for its expansion and modernisation. Plan I demanded that modern aircraft be built immediately and called for follow-up designs. Among these was the **LeO 45**, a 'fast heavy bomber capable of being operated by day or night at medium altitude'. Powered by Hispano-Suiza 14 radials, the prototype **LeO 45-01** flew on 16 January 1937, but these engines gave constant trouble and were switched to Gnome-Rhône 14N radials in production aircraft. At the outbreak of war 749 **LeO 451**s (and derivatives) were on order but only 10 were on Armée de l'Air charge. First unit to equip was GB I/31, followed by GB I/12 and II./12, and these were still the only units that had completely re-equipped when the Germans launched their major attack on 10 May 1940. From the outset the LeO 451s were operated in a manner for which they were unsuited, i.e. low-level ground support in the presence of enemy air opposition. As such, the aircraft suffered heavy losses, although new units were formed and replacements delivered. By the end of the Battle of France, 373 LeO 451s and derivatives had been

delivered to the Armée de l'Air and Aéronavale, which had lost 150. Production continued in unoccupied France, and the LeO 451 served in North Africa and Syria with the Vichy forces. Some were flown against the Allies in these theatres.

Lioré et Olivier LeO 451

Specification: Lioré et Olivier LeO 451
Type: four-crew bomber
Powerplant: two 1,060-hp (791-KW) Gnome-Rhône 14N 48/49 radial pistons
Performance: max speed 298 mph (480 km/h) at 15,750 ft (4800 m); service ceiling 29,530 ft (9000 m); range 1,802 miles (2900 km)
Weights: empty 16,600 lb (7530 kg); max take-off 25,132 lb (11400 kg)
Dimensions: span 73 ft 10½ in (22.52 m); length 56 ft 4 in (17.17 m); height 17 ft 2¼ in (5.24 m); wing area 710.4 sq ft (66.00 m²)
Armament: one fixed forward-firing plus (in retractable gondola) two rearward-firing 7.5-mm (0.295-in) MAC 1934 M39 guns, one dorsal 20-mm H5404 cannon; max bomb load (with reduced fuel) 3,086 lb (1400 kg)

After the Torch landings of November 1942, the Germans invaded the Unoccupied Zone of France and seized 94 LeO 451s, many of which were impressed into service. Variants with different engines reached prototype form, some production aircraft being modified as transports, glider tugs, mailplanes and trainers.

Lockheed P-38 Lightning

Neutral air forces in Europe reaped a harvest of the aircraft which landed in their territory. This USAAF P-38 was one that landed at Lisbon, Portugal, while flying from Britain to North Africa in 1943, and was impressed into service.

Lockheed's first military aircraft, the twin-engined, twin-boom **P-38 Lightning** was designed to meet a 1937 requirement for a high-altitude interceptor. First flown on 27 January 1939, the **XP-38** was followed by production P-38s with nose armament of one 37-mm and four 0.5-in (12.7-mm) guns and were powered by Allison V-1710-27/29s; their top speed of 390 mph (628 km/h) was greater than any other American fighter in 1941. The first version to be considered fully operational was the **P-38D**, which reached squadrons at the time of Pearl Harbor. The first of an RAF order for 143 aircraft arrived in the UK in December 1941, but after evaluation they were rejected (due to a ban imposed on the export of turbochargers) and the contract cancelled. In the USAAF the P-38D was followed by the **P-38E**, in which the 37-mm cannon was replaced by a 20-mm weapon. The **P-38F**, with a bomb load of up to 2,000 lb (907 kg) under the wings, was followed by the **P-38G** with minor equipment changes. The **P-38H** could carry up to 3,200 lb (1452 kg) of bombs. In the **P-38J** (2,970 produced), the radiators were located in deep 'chin' fairings aft of the propellers; with maximum external fuel load this version had an endurance of about 12 hours. In a P-38 America's top-scoring fighter pilot, Major Richard I. Bong, gained most of his 40 victories. The **P-38L** was the most-built version (3,923) and had -111/113 engines in place of the P-38J's -89/91s. **F-4** and **F-5** photo-reconnaissance conversions were used in Europe and the Far East.

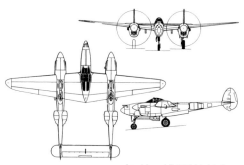

Lockheed P-38J Lightning

The P-38 gave excellent service in Europe as a long-range fighter and photo-reconnaissance aircraft, but the vast distances involved in the Pacific war and the increasing inferiority of Japanese aircraft represented the ideal scenario for this fast, hard-hitting, twin-engined fighter. Production of all Lightnings totalled 9,394.

Specification:
Lockheed P-38L Lightning
Type: single-seat fighter/fighter-bomber
Powerplant: two 1,475-hp (1100-kW) Allison V-1710-111/113 inline pistons
Performance: max speed 414 mph (666 km/h) at 25,000 ft (7620 m); climb to 20,000 ft (6095 m) in 7.0 minutes; service ceiling 44,000 ft (13410 m); range 450 miles (724 km)
Weights: empty 12,800 lb (5806 kg); max take-off 21,600 lb (9798 kg)
Dimensions: span 52 ft 0 in (15.85 m); length 37 ft 10 in (11.52 m); height 9 ft 10 in (2.99 m); wing area 327.5 sq ft (30.42 m²)
Armament: one 20-mm and four 0.5-in (12.7-mm) guns in nose; up to two 1,600-lb (726-kg) bombs under wings

Lockheed 14 (A-28/-29)

This Lockheed Hudson Mk V is seen in mid-war RAF markings. A total of 409 Mk Vs was delivered to the RAF from 1941, and the aircraft shown, AM579, was one of those flown directly from California to Auckland, New Zealand.

Originating in 1938, the **Lockheed Hudson** grew from a request that the **Lockheed 14** transport be developed as a maritime reconnaissance aircraft. The first aircraft was flown on 10 December 1938, and the first to arrive in the UK was disembarked at Liverpool on 15 February 1939. After the initiation of the Lend-Lease programme the aircraft were given the US designation **A-28** and **A-28A**, some of the British aircraft being repossessed as **A-29**s and **A-29A**s by the USAAF after Pearl Harbor. The first U-boat to be sunk by American forces was attacked by an A-29 of the 13th Bomb Group. The **AT-18** was an attack trainer version (with dorsal turret removed, the **AT-18B**). It was in the RAF that the aircraft saw most service. The original order for 200 (soon increased to 350) aircraft were designated **Hudson Mk I**s; hydromatic propellers identified the **Mk II.**, and the **Mk III** was powered by 1,200-hp (985-kW) Wright GR-1820 G205A radials. Hudsons entered service with the RAF's No. 224 Squadron in mid-1939, replacing Avro Ansons, and thereafter flew constant patrols over the North Sea; after the arrival of the Mk III with extra fuel tanks, the aircraft participated in the Battle of the Atlantic. It was the crew of a No. 269 Squadron Hudson to whom the U-boat U-570 surrendered after an attack on 27 August 1941. Final versions were the Hudson **Mks IV**, **V** and **VI** with Pratt & Whitney radials. Hudsons equipped 31 RAF squadrons, serving as transports at the war's end.

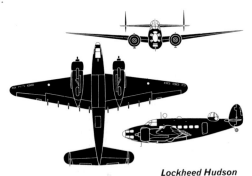

Lockheed Hudson

Specification: Lockheed A-29 (Hudson Mk IIIA)
Type: four-crew bomber
Powerplant: two 1,200-hp (895-kW) Wright R-1820-87 radial pistons
Performance: max speed 253 mph (407 km/h) at 15,000 ft (4570 m); climb to 10,000 ft (3050 m) in 6.3 minutes; service ceiling 26,500 ft (8075 m); range 1,550 miles (2494 km)
Weights: empty 12,825 lb (5817 kg); max take-off 20,500 lb (9299 kg)
Dimensions: span 65 ft 6 in (19.96 m); length 44 ft 4 in (13.51 m); height 11 ft 11 in (3.63 m); wing area 551.0 sq ft (51.19 m²)
Armament: two fixed forward-firing 0.3-in (7.62-mm) guns in nose, one 0.3-in (7.62-mm) gun each in ventral position and dorsal turret; bomb load 1,600 lb (726 kg)

In American service the Lockheed A-28 and A-29 were used for duties such as anti-submarine patrol, photo reconnaissance, troop-carrying, crew training and target-towing. A total of 2,487 Hudsons was purchased by Britain, 423 being supplied to Canada, South Africa, China, New Zealand, Australia and Portugal.

Macchi C.200 Saetta

This early C.200 Saetta of the 371ª Squadriglia CT, 22º Gruppo CT, based in Albania in March 1941, sports a Cucaracha (cockroach) emblem on the rear fuselage. This unit later took its Saettas to the Eastern Front to support the offensive on the Dnieper.

Handicapped by Italy's pre-war lack of an inline engine suitable for fighters, the Fiat radial-powered **Macchi C.200** was, in 1939, already outclassed by 1937's Hurricane. The first C.200 unit, the 4º Stormo, even expressed a preference for the CR.42 and accordingly reverted to the biplane in 1940. First flown on 24 December 1937 by Giuseppe Burei, the C.200, named **Saetta** (Lightning), went on to equip the 1º, 2º, 3º, 4º (in mid-1941) and 54º Stormi, and the 8º, 12º, 13º, 21º and 22º Gruppi, about 1,200 aircraft being produced by Macchi, Breda and SAI Ambrosini. When Italy entered the war on 10 June 1940, two home-based *stormi* were combat-ready with the C.200, being first flown in action over Malta in September that year, and it was largely the Italian losses suffered then and during the Greek campaign that prompted the Luftwaffe to deploy X Fliegerkorps in the Mediterranean to bolster the Regia Aeronautica's flagging resources. C.200s were heavily committed in North Africa, and were fairly evenly matched with the early Hurricane Mk Is, weighed down by tropical air filters, but the attrition suffered by all Italian air force units (principally through poor serviceability and attacks on their air fields) quickly reduced the number of C.200s. Some 51 Saettas of the 22º Gruppo operated in the Odessa Zone of the Russian Front from August 1941, proving capable of matching almost any Russian fighter. By the time of the Italian armistice in September 1943, the number of serviceable C.200s stood at only 33.

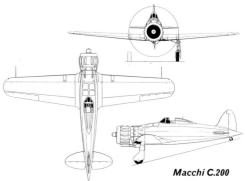

Macchi C.200

This Macchi C.200 taxis down the field to a dispersal area. Generally regarded as marginally better than the Fiat G.50, the C.200 survived in front-line service until 1943, although by then it was wholly outclassed by mid-war Allied fighters in the Mediterranean theatre, and its gun armament was inadequate to combat bombers.

Specification: Macchi C.200 Saetta (Breda-built Series 6)
Type: single-seat fighter/fighter-bomber
Powerplant: one 870-hp (649-kW) Fiat A.74 RC 38 radial piston
Performance: max speed 313 mph (504 km/h) at 14,765 ft (4500 m); climb to 13,125 ft (4000 m) in 4.55 minutes; service ceiling 29,200 ft (8900 m); range 354 miles (570 km)
Weights: empty 4,321 lb (1960 kg); max take-off 5,280 lb (2395 kg)
Dimensions: span 34 ft 8½ in (10.58 m); length 27 ft 0¾ in (8.25 m); height 10 ft 0⅛ in (3.05 m); wing area 180.8 sq ft (16.80 m²)
Armament: two 12.7-mm (0.5-in) Breda SAFAT machine-guns in nose; two 331-lb (50-kg) bombs

Macchi C.202 Folgore/C.205

Following the Italian armistice of September 1943, a relatively small number of Macchi C.205V Veltro fighters joined the Co-Belligerent Air Force, but their service was not prolonged. This C.205V served with the 155º Gruppo, 51º Stormo at Lecce late in 1944.

One of the best Italian fighters of the mid-war years, Mario Castoldi's **Macchi C.202 Folgore** (Thunderbolt) was developed from the radial-powered C.200, but was powered by a Daimler-Benz DB.601 produced under licence as the Alfa Romeo RA 1000 RC 411. First flown by Carestiato on 10 August 1940, the **C.202 Series I** production version entered service with the 1º Stormo at Udine in the summer of 1941, this unit arriving in Libya in the following November. The Folgore was a low-wing monoplane with inward-retracting landing gear and an armament of two 12.7-mm (0.5-in) Breda SAFAT machine-guns in the nose; there was also provision for two 7.7-mm (0.303-in) guns in the wings. Engine production was slow and severely delayed the build-up of the type in service. The aircraft underwent very little change and development during its life span, and was produced in 11 series. It eventually served with 45 *squadriglie* of the 1º, 2º, 3º, 4º, 51º, 52º, 53º and 54º Stormi in North Africa, Sicily, Italy, the Aegean and Russia. Production amounted to about 1,500, of which 392 were produced by the parent company and the remainder by Breda. In combat, the Folgore proved to be well matched with the Spitfire Mk V in performance but was badly under-gunned and, although certainly superior to American fighters such as the P-39 Airacobra, this armament deficiency prevented Folgore pilots from knocking down many Allied bombers.

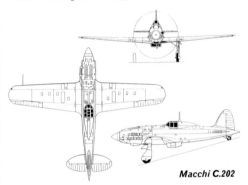

Macchi C.202

Specification: Macchi C.202 Series IX Folgore
Type: single-seat fighter
Powerplant: one 1,075-hp (802-kW) Alfa Romeo RA 1000 RC 411 inline piston
Performance: max speed 373 mph (600 km/h) at 18,375 ft (5600 m); climb to 16,405 ft (5000 m) in 4.6 minutes; service ceiling 37,730 ft (11500 m); range 379 miles (610 km)
Weights: empty 5,489 lb (2490 kg); max take-off 6,459 lb (2930 kg)
Dimensions: span 34 ft 8½ in (10.58 m); length 29 ft 1½ in (8.85 m); height 11 ft 5½ in (3.50 m); wing area 180.8 sq ft (16.80 m²)
Armament: two 12.7-mm (0.5-in) Breda SAFAT machine-guns in nose; two 7.7-mm (0.303-in) guns in wings

Ultimate wartime development of the C.200/202 series of Italian fighters was the Daimler-Benz-powered C.205 Veltro (Greyhound), seen here. The type became operational in mid-1943 and was regarded as the best Italian fighter of the war, combining performance with agility and firepower.

Martin 167 Maryland

Apart from six squadrons of the RAF, a number of Commonwealth squadrons also flew the Maryland. The aircraft shown here belonged to No. 24 Sqn, South African Air Force, based at Fuka, Egypt, in May 1941.

Developed as the US Army Air Corps' XA-22 attack bomber, the **Martin 167 Maryland** failed to gain acceptance by the Americans after its first flight on 14 March 1938. Promises of quick delivery attracted the French, who ordered 175 aircraft (the **Martin 167F**) for delivery by the end of 1940. About 75 of these had been delivered before France surrendered to the Germans in June that year, two units (GB I/62 and I/63) having flown the aircraft during the brief Battle of France; about 60 of these subsequently served with Vichy forces in North Africa and Syria, and in due course were flown in action against the Allies. Some of the survivors from the debacle in France were flown to the UK and served with the RAF, while the UK itself ordered another 150 aircraft as **Maryland Mk II**s with two-stage supercharged engines, to join 75 Maryland **Mk I**s (Martin 167Fs with single-stage supercharged engines diverted from the French order). Most of these 225 aircraft were flown or shipped to the Middle East, first serving on No. 431 General Reconnaissance Flight at Malta in October 1940. It was one of these aircraft that made the famous reconnaissance fight over Taranto harbour before the brilliant attack by Swordfish that temporarily crippled the Italian battle fleet. In due course Marylands equipped three RAF bomber squadrons and four of the South African Air Force, all in the Mediterranean theatre.

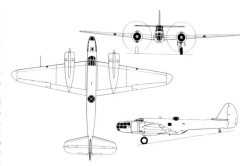

Martin Maryland I

Originating in a French rather than a British order, the Martin Maryland entered service with the RAF in 1940. One of its memorable exploits was a low-level reconnaissance of Taranto harbour prior to the devastating attack by Fleet Air Arm Swordfish torpedo-bombers.

Specification: Martin 167 Maryland Mk II
Type: three-crew reconnaissance bomber
Powerplant: two 1,200-hp (895-kW) Pratt & Whitney S3C4-G radial pistons
Performance: max speed 278 mph (448 km/h) at 11,800 ft (3595 m); climb rate 1,790 ft (546 m) per minute; ceiling 26,000 ft (7925 m); range with bomb load 1,210 miles (1947 km)
Weights: empty 11,213 lb (5086 kg); max take-off 16,809 lb (7631 kg)
Dimensions: span 61 ft 4 in (18.69 m); length 46 ft 8 in (14.22 m); height 14 ft 11¼ in (4.55 m); wing area 538.5 sq ft (50.03 m²)
Armament: four 0.303-in (7.7-mm) machine-guns in wings, single 0.303-in (7.7-mm) flexible guns in dorsal turret and ventral positions; bomb load 2,000 lb (901 kg)

Martin 187 Baltimore

This ex-USAAF Martin A-30A-10-MA Baltimore Mk V, FW332, is from No. 232 Wing, North-west African Tactical Air Force. Comprising Nos 55 and 223 Sqns, the wing flew the Mk V in the 1944 Italian campaign.

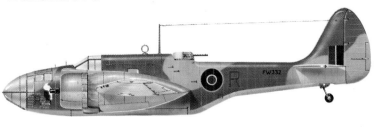

One of the reasons given by the British Purchasing Mission in America for not selecting the Martin 167 bomber was the lack of direct communication between the two front crew members and the rear gunner. In 1940, however, otherwise impressed with the performance of the aircraft purchased by France, the British requested a new version with a deeper fuselage allowing direct access between all crew members (increased to four). The prototype **Martin 187** was flown on 14 June 1941, and although designated **A-30** by the USAAF none was in fact delivered for American use. Apart from the prototype, which arrived in the UK during October 1941, deliveries started with 50 **Baltimore Mk I**s in 1942 with 1,600-hp (1194-kW) Wright R-2600-A5B radials and a single machine-gun in the dorsal position; 100 **Mk II**s followed with twin dorsal guns but were otherwise similar; 250 **Mk III**s, with power-operated Boulton Paul dorsal turret and R-2600-19 engines, completed the initial order for 400 aircraft. After the negotiation of Lend-Lease, 281 additional **Mk III**s were supplied as **Mk IIIA**s, followed by 294 **Mk IV**s with a Martin dorsal turret. Finally, 600 **Mk V**s with 1,700-hp (1268-kW)

R-2600-29 engines brought the total of RAF deliveries to 1,575. From March 1942 until the end of the war these aircraft gave magnificent service in North Africa, Sicily and Italy; some were passed to the Italian Co-Belligerent Forces and were used by the Stormo Baltimore over the Balkans in 1945.

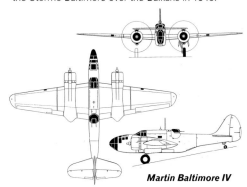

Martin Baltimore IV

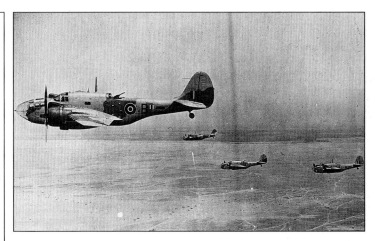

This Baltimore Mk II is seen with three other Baltimores during the conflict in the South Desert. All RAF Baltimores (of which 1,575 were delivered) were employed in the Mediterranean theatre, equipping seven RAF and two SAAF squadrons.

Martin B-26 Marauder

Marauders served on only two RAF squadrons: the short-span Marauder Mk I depicted here flew with No.14 Sqn in North Africa from August 1942 to September 1944, and later the long-span Marauder Mk III served on No. 39 Sqn.

Frequently associated with dangerous low-speed handling characteristics (a reflection more on inadequate training than faulty design), the **Martin B-26** was one of the outstanding medium/light bombers of the war. Under the design leadership of Peyton M. Magruder, the Martin 179 was submitted to the US Army Board on 5 July 1939, and 1,100 aircraft were ordered two months later. The first development B-26 was flown on 25 November 1940. Deliveries to the USAAF began in 1941, accompanied by a spate of accidents during pilot conversion. **B-26A**s first equipped the 22nd Bomb Group, which took its new aircraft to Australia on the day that Japan attacked Pearl Harbor; the aircraft were first flown into action over New Guinea in April 1942. The **B-26B** introduced increased armour and improved gun armament, while later sub-variants featured increased wingspan in an attempt to reduce the landing approach speed, but this was largely offset by an increase in the gross weight. A total of 1,883 B-26Bs was produced at Martin's Baltimore plant and 1,235 **B-26C**s (similar to the B-26B) at Omaha, Nebraska. The first B-26s arrived in the UK in February 1943 but suffered heavy losses in early raids. Subsequent versions included the **B-26F** and **B-26G** with wing incidence increased by 3.5° in an attempt to improve take-off performance. Total production reached 5,157 aircraft, including 522 which served in the RAF and SAAF in the Mediterranean.

Martin B-26 Marauder

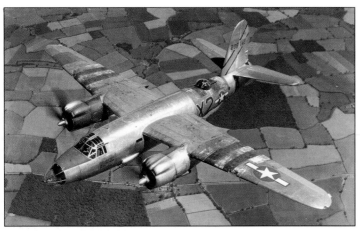

Although frequently criticised on account of its tricky handling qualities, the B-26 packed a heavy punch and was widely used by the USAAF in Europe. This B-26B of the 593th Bomb Squadron, 397th Bomb Wing, has had its 'invasion stripes' deliberately toned down in the interests of camouflage.

Specification: Martin B-26C Marauder
Type: seven-crew medium/light bomber
Powerplant: two 2,000-hp (1492-kW) Pratt & Whitney R-2800-43 radial pistons
Performance: max speed 282 mph (454 km/h) at 15,000 ft (4570 m); climb to 15,000 ft (4570 m) in 24.5 minutes; service ceiling 21,700 ft (6615 m); range 1,150 miles (1850 km)
Weights: empty 22,380 lb (10152 kg); max take-off 34,200 lb (15513 kg)
Dimensions: span 71 ft 0 in (21.64 m); length 58 ft 3 in (17.75 m); height 20 ft 4 in (6.20 m); wing area 658.0 sq ft (61.13 m²)
Armament: 12 0.5-in (12.7-mm) machine-guns (two in nose, four on fuselage sides, two in dorsal turret, two in ventral position, two in tail); bomb load 3,000 lb (1361 kg)

Messerschmitt Bf 109

This Messerschmitt Bf 109E-3 was flown by Hauptmann Henschel, Gruppenkommandeur, II./JG 77, which was based at Aalborg, Norway in July 1940. JG 77 at Aalborg was also involved with night-fighting using Bf 109Cs.

First flown in September 1935, Willy Messerschmitt's single-seat **Bf 109** fighter saw action during the Spanish Civil War in the **Bf 109B** version (Junkers Jumo 210 engine). It joined the Luftwaffe in 1937 and was followed by the **Bf 109C** with armament increased from three to four rifle-calibre machine-guns. The **Bf 109D** introduced the Daimler-Benz DB 600 engine and hub-firing cannon, and was produced in 1938-39. First major production variant was the **Bf 109E** with DB 601D engine and direct fuel injection, and variations of armament between two machine-guns, and four machine-guns, and one hub cannon. Fighter-bomber and reconnaissance versions were produced during 1940. The **Bf 109E** was the Luftwaffe's principal fighter during 1939-40. It was followed by the **Bf 109F**, powered initially by the DB 601N and later the DB 601E, and introduced such equipment as nitrous-oxide power boosting, faster-firing guns (15-mm MG 151) and optional under-wing gun pods. Both the Bf 109E and Bf 109F existed in tropicalised form for service in North Africa during 1941-42. The **Bf 109G**, with DB 605 engine, served from 1942 until 1945, being built in the largest numbers and introducing such armament as 30-mm guns. Fastest of all was the **Bf 109G-10** (429 mph/690 km/h). The final main production version was the **Bf 109K** with boosted DB 605s. Other versions included the high-altitude **Bf 109H** and shipboard **Bf 109T** fighters.

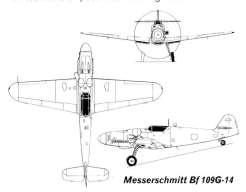

Messerschmitt Bf 109G-14

Specification:
Messerschmitt Bf 109G-6
Type: single-seat interceptor fighter
Powerplant: one 1,475-hp (1100-kW) Daimler-Benz DB 605A inline piston
Performance: max speed 387 mph (623 km/h) at 22,965 ft (7000 m); climb to 19,685 ft (6000 m) in 6.0 minutes; service ceiling 38,550 ft (11750 m); range 450 miles (725 km)
Weights: empty 5,952 lb (2700 kg); max take-off 6,944 lb (3150 kg)
Dimensions: span 32 ft 6½ in (9.92 m); length 29 ft 7 in (9.02 m); height 11 ft 2 in (3.40 m); wing area 172.8 sq ft (16.05 m²)
Armament: two nose-mounted 7.92-mm (0.31-in) MG 17 guns, one hub-firing 30-mm MK 108 cannon, two 20-mm MG 151/20 cannon mounted under wings

The Messerschmitt Bf 109E-4 Trop fighters of 1./Jagdgeschwader 27 brought a new tactical dimension to air operations over North Africa, as they clearly outclassed all available British fighters in that theatre in spring 1941. More than 33,000 Bf 109s were built between 1937 and 1945.

Messerschmitt Bf 110

This Messerschmitt Bf 110C of the Stabsschwarm (staff flight) belonged to I./Zerstörergeschwader 2, based at Amiens during July 1940. The type failed against the RAF's Spitfires and Hurricanes.

The **Messerschmitt Bf 110** was conceived in 1934 and first flown on 12 May 1936; pre-production **Bf 110A-0s** followed in 1937-38 with Junkers Jumo 210B engines. Production started with the **Bf 110B** in 1938 with Jumo 210Gs and forward armament of two 20-mm and four 7.92-mm (0.31-in) guns, plus one 7.92-mm (0.31-in) gun in the rear cockpit. Daimler-Benz DB 601A-powered **Bf 110Cs** joined the Luftwaffe in 1939 in time for the attack on Poland, and were employed as fighters and fighter-bombers throughout 1940. The **Bf 110C-5** was a reconnaissance version. The long-range **Bf 110D** entered service in 1940, and sub-variants were the first Bf 110s to be employed as night-fighters. There were also tropicalised and fighter-bomber versions. The **Bf 110E** fighter-bomber was powered by DB 601Ns and the **Bf 110F** by DB 601Es. Despite its high top speed, the Bf 110 was quickly shown to be no match for opposing single-engined fighters, and from 1941 development was confined mainly to ground attack and night-fighter versions. The **Bf 110F-4** introduced two 30-mm guns under the fuselage, and the **Bf 110F-4/U1** featured twin upward-firing 20-mm guns in a *schrage Musik* installation. **Bf 110Gs** with DB 605Bs were produced in *Zerstörer*, fighter-bomber, reconnaissance and night-fighter versions, and sub-variants introduced the 37-mm underfuselage gun. Radar-equipped **Bf 110Gs** were the Luftwaffe's principal night-fighter in 1943-1945, and participated in daylight battles over Germany.

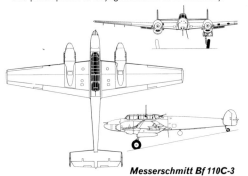

Messerschmitt Bf 110C-3

Messerschmitt Bf 110s were of great use to the Luftwaffe in the Mediterranean, where the type's great range and tactical flexibility proved a decided advantage. The type was Germany's first attempt at a twin-engined two-seat 'heavy fighter' (or Zerstörer, destroyer).

Specification:
Messerschmitt Bf 110C-4
Type: two-seat heavy fighter
Powerplant: two 1,100-hp (821-kW) Daimler-Benz DB 601A inline pistons
Performance: max speed 349 mph (560 km/h) at 22,965 ft (7000 m); initial climb rate 2,165 ft (660 m) per minute; service ceiling 32,810 ft (10000 m); normal range 482 miles (775 km)
Weights: empty 11,464 lb (5200 kg); max take-off 14,881 lb (6750 kg)
Dimensions: span 53 ft 4¾ in (16.27 m); length 41 ft 6¾ in (12.65 m); height 11 ft 6 in (3.50 m); wing area 413.3 sq ft (38.40 m²)
Armament: two 20-mm MG 151 cannon and four 7.92-mm (0.31-in) MG 17 guns in nose, firing forward, and one 7.92-mm (0.31-in) MG 81Z twin gun on flexible mounting in rear cockpit firing aft

Messerschmitt Me 163 Komet

This Me 163B-1 wears the unit badge of JG 400 – a rocket-powered flea. The two letter stencils on the aircraft's back denote the fuelling points for the two separate fuels (C-Stoff and T-Stoff), contact between which could result in fatal accidents.

The **Messerschmitt Me 163 Komet** (Comet) prototype was test flown as a glider during the spring of 1941 before fitment with a Walter RII-203 rocket using *T-Stoff* and *Z-Stoff* fuels. Powered flights by the **Me 163V1** started in the summer of 1941, and on 2 October the aircraft reached 623.8 mph (1004.5 km/h). Production **Me 163B**s were powered by Walter 109-509A rocket motors using *T-Stoff* (hydrogen peroxide) and *C-Stoff* (hydrazine hydrate, methyl alcohol and water) to give a thrust of 3,748 lb (16.67 kN). Early **Me 163B-0**s were armed with a pair of 20-mm guns, but **Me 163B-1**s carried two 30-mm weapons. The aircraft had no conventional landing gear, but took off from a trolley which was jettisoned immediately after take-off. Introduction to service was a protracted and hazardous process owing to difficulties in handling the fuels (and a number of fatal accidents) and only very experienced pilots were selected. Production **Me 163B-1a** fighters equipped I./JG 400 at Brandis in June 1944 and first intercepted B-17 Fortress daylight bombers on 16 August. Many difficulties faced the pilots apart from those already mentioned, and it was difficult to aim and fire the guns so upward-firing 50-mm shells and underwing rockets came to be developed. Although 300 Me 163Bs were produced (in addition to a number of **Me 163C**s with increased fuel), and JG 400's other two *Gruppen* re-equipped by the end of 1944, only nine confirmed air victories were achieved by the *Geschwader*.

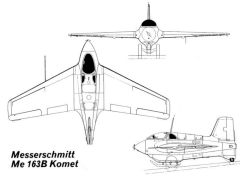

Messerschmitt Me 163B Komet

Specification:
Messerschmitt Me 163B-1a Komet
Type: single-seat interceptor fighter
Powerplant: one 3,748-lb (16.67-kN) thrust Walter 109-509A-2 rocket motor
Performance: max speed 596 mph (960 km/h) at 9,845 ft (3000 m); initial climb rate 11,810 ft (3600 m) per minute; service ceiling 39,700 ft (12100 m); normal range 50 miles (80 km)
Weights: empty 4,200 lb (1905 kg); max take-off 9,061 lb (4110 kg)
Dimensions: span 30 ft 7¼ in (9.33 m); length 18 ft 8 in (5.69 m); height 9 ft 0½ (2.76 m); wing area 211.2 sq ft (19.62 m²)
Armament: two 30-mm MK 108 cannon

This Me 163 Komet is from JG 400, the only unit to fly the extraordinary little fighter. The two-wheeled trolley on which the aircraft stands would have been jettisoned on take-off, the Komet then alighting on its skid after its short sortie. Dr Alexander Lippisch had researched the rocket interceptor for 15 years.

Messerschmitt Me 210/Me 410 Hornisse

One of the first units to receive the Messerschmitt Me 410A Hornisse (Hornet) was III. Gruppe, Zerstörergeschwader 1, in May 1943. This Me 410A-1 was flown by 9. Staffel from Gerbini.

Conceived in 1937, the **Messerschmitt Me 210V1** prototype was flown on 2 September 1939 with twin fins and rudders, and was powered by two Daimler-Benz DB 601Aa engines. Production **Me 210A-1**s joined the Luftwaffe in 1941 and were armed with two 20-mm forward-firing guns and two 7.92-mm (0.31-in) guns in remotely-controlled barbettes on the sides of the fuselage, firing aft. Variants included the **Me 210A-2** fighter-bomber, the **Me 210B-1** photo reconnaissance aircraft and the **Me 210C** and **Me 210D** with 1,475-hp (1100-kW) DB 605B engines. As a result of continuing handling difficulties, Me 210 development was halted in 1942 and design effort was concentrated on the **Me 410 Hornisse** (Hornet), powered by two DB 603A engines. A prototype flew at the end of the year and was followed by **Me 410A-1** light bombers armed with two 20-mm and two 7.92-mm (0.31-in) guns in the nose and two guns in the barbettes; it could also carry two 2,205-lb (1000-kg) bombs internally. Variants included the **Me 410A-1/U1** photo-reconnaissance aircraft and the **Me 410A-1/U4** bomber-destroyer with a single 50-mm gun (with 21 rounds) under the fuselage.

The light bombers were used against the British Isles from 1943. The **Me 410B** appeared in 1944, with two 1,900-hp (1417-kW) DB 603Gs. Sub-variants included a torpedo fighter (**Me 410B-5**) and an anti-shipping fighter (**Me 410B-6**) with a forward armament of two 30-mm, two 20-mm and two 13-mm guns, as well as FuG 200 Hohentweil radar.

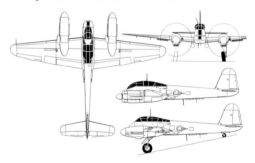

Messerschmitt Me 410A-1 (upper view: Me 410D)

The excellent Messerschmitt Me 410 was produced to perform a number of different duties. This Me 410A-3 of 2. Staffel, Aufklarungsgruppe 122, was based at Trapani in May 1943 for specialist photo-reconnaissance. Production ceased in September 1944 after 1,160 had been produced.

Specification:
Messerschmitt Me 410A-1 /U2
Type: two-seat heavy fighter
Powerplant: two 1,750-hp (1305-KW) Daimler-Benz DB 603A inlines
Performance: max speed 388 mph (625 km/h) at 21,980 ft (6700 m); climb to 21,980 ft (6700 m) in 10.7 minutes; service ceiling 32,810 ft (10000 m); range 1,448 miles (2330 km)
Weights: empty 13,558 lb (6150 kg); max take-off 23,483 lb (10650 kg)
Dimensions: span 53 ft 7¾ in (16.35 m); length 40 ft 8½ in (12.40 m); height 14 ft 0½ in (4.28 m); wing area 389.7 sq ft (36.20 m²)
Armament: four 20-mm MG 151/20 and two 7.92-mm (0.31-in) MG 17 forward-firing guns, and two 13-mm (0.51-in) MG 131 guns in rear barbettes

Messerschmitt Me 262

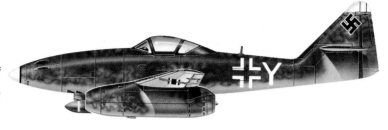

A Messerschmitt Me 262A-2a bomber. By persisting with bomber development on Hitler's direction, the Luftwaffe was deprived of this remarkable fighter until late 1944. This example served with I./KG 51 at Achmer in spring 1945.

The **Messerschmitt Me 262** was the world's first turbojet-powered aircraft to achieve combat status. Design of the aircraft started in 1938 and prototype airframes were ready in 1941 but, as the Junkers jet engines were not then ready, the first flight on 18 April was made using a single Jumo 210G piston engine; it was not until 18 July 1942 that the **Me 262V3** first made an all-jet flight powered by two 1,852-lb (8.24-kN) thrust Junkers 109-004A-0 turbojets. Early prototypes featured tailwheel landing gear, but when production started in 1944 a tricycle arrangement had been standardised. As Hitler persisted in demanding development of the Me 262 as a bomber, development of the fighter was badly delayed and it did not enter service until late in 1944. The **Me 262A-1a Schwalbe** (Swallow) fighter was armed with four 30-mm guns in the nose and joined Kommando Nowotny in October. The **Me 262A-1a/U1** had two additional 20-mm guns, the **Me 262A-1a/U2** was a bad weather fighter and the **Me 262A-1a/U3** an unarmed reconnaissance aircraft. The **Me 262A-2a Sturmvogel** (Stormy Petrel) bomber could carry up to 2,205 lb (1000 kg) of bombs in addition to the four 30-mm guns; the **Me 262A-2a/U2** was a two-seat version (with prone bomb aimer). Me 262s flew with some success against Allied bombers both as day and night-fighters (the latter were radar-equipped Me 262B-1a/U1s), and air-to-air rockets were being developed.

Messerschmitt Me 262A-1a

Specification:
Messerschmitt Me 262A-1a
Type: single-seat interceptor fighter
Powerplant: two 1,984-lb (8.83-kN) thrust Junkers Jumo 109-004B-4 turbojets
Performance: max speed 541 mph (870 km/h) at 22,965 ft (7000 m); initial climb rate 3,937 ft (1200 m) per minute; service ceiling 36,090 ft (11000 m); normal range 525 miles (845 km)
Weights: empty 8,818 lb (4000 kg); max take-off 14,936 lb (6775 kg)
Dimensions: span 41 ft 0⅛ in (12.50 m); length 34 ft 9½ in (10.61 m); height 12 ft 6¾ in (3.83 m); wing area 233.3 sq ft (21.68 m²)
Armament: four 30-mm MK 108 cannon in nose

The Me 262 was a cantilever low-wing monoplane with its engines nacelle-mounted below the wing. Dogged by difficulties brought on by Allied raids on factories and airfields, the Luftwaffe's jet fighter units nevertheless posed a formidable threat to Allied air superiority during the last few months of the war.

Messerschmitt Me 323

Owing to its obvious vulnerability, the Me 323 was not employed as an assault aircraft but was used for heavy-lift duties behind the front line. This Me 323E of I./TG 5 served behind the Southern Sector of the Russian Front in late 1943.

The first prototype **Me 323V1** (a fully-powered version of the Me 321 Gigant glider) had four 1,140-hp (850-kW) Gnome-Rhône 14N radials when it first flew in May 1942, but proved to be so underpowered that the **Me 323V3** was fitted with six of the same engines. The first production version, the **Me 323D-1**, appeared in September 1942 and featured defensive armament of five 7.92-mm (0.31-in) guns in the nose and up to 10 7.92-mm (0.31-in) guns in the fuselage sides. Four months later the **Me 323D-5** appeared with the nose guns increased to 13-mm (0.51-in) calibre; this had a crew of five and normally carried up to 130 troops. **Me 323DF-1**s first joined Kampfgruppe zur besonderen Verwendung 323 in Sicily in November 1942, and were later joined by **Me 323D-6**s. They were heavily committed during the evacuation of the German forces in North Africa but suffered badly under Allied fighters. Later versions included the **Me 323E-1** with 1,200-hp (895-kW) Gnome-Rhône 14N engines and gun turrets (each with a 20-mm gun) in the top of each wing, and the **Me 323E-3** with 1,340-hp (1000-kW) Junkers Jumo engines, a nose gun turret and four 13-mm (0.51-in) guns in

the rear of the inboard and outboard engine nacelles. Early in 1944 Me 323s joined I. and II./TG 5 on the Eastern Front, part of the large German air transport fleet supplying the German armies falling back before the advancing Russians. The Me 323 was a remarkable aircraft, but its use in conditions of enemy air superiority resulted in heavy losses.

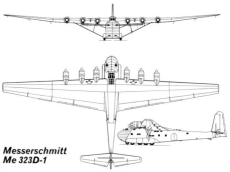

Messerschmitt Me 323D-1

The first six-engined prototype of the Me 323 proved to have sufficient power but its performance margin was slight, necessitating still more powerful engines for production versions. Structure of this huge aircraft was steel tubing and wood, with wood and fabric covering. A total of 198 was produced.

Specification:
Messerschmitt Me 323D-6
Type: five-crew heavy military transport
Powerplant: six 1,600-hp (1194-kW) BMW 801A radial pistons
Performance: max speed 177 mph (285 km/h) at sea level; initial climb rate 708 ft (216 m) per minute; range 683 miles (1100 km)
Weights: empty 60,251 lb (27330 kg); max take-off 94,797 lb (43000 kg)
Dimensions: span 180 ft 5½ in (55.00 m); length 92 ft 4¼ in (28.15 m); height 31 ft 6 in (9.60 m); wing area 3,229.3 sq ft (300.0 m²)
Accommodation and armament: 130 fully-armed troops or up to 35,030 lb (15890 kg) of military stores; defensive armament of five 13-mm (0.51-in) and 10 7.92-mm (0.31-in) machine-guns

Mikoyan-Gurevich MiG-3

This MiG-3 of the 34th Fighter Aviation Regiment, IA-PVO, based at Vnukovo, is seen probably early in 1943. Due to handling problems, the MiG-3 was no match for German fighters such as the Bf 109G that took a heavy toll of Soviet aircraft in the mid-war years.

Gaining a reputation as a 'hot ship' in the mid-war years, Artem Mikoyan's **MiG-3** was plagued by difficult handling and very poor armament and, although among the fastest of Russian fighters of that period, it proved no match for the German Bf 109G or Fw 190. Flown in prototype form as the **I-61** in the spring of 1940, the initial design included the 1,200-hp (895-kW) Mikulin AM-35 inline engine, and this was retained in the production MiG-1, which began to appear in September 1940. Handicapped by the overall length of the engine – which seems to have resulted in poor directional stability – and armed with only three machine-guns, the MiG-1 suffered heavily in the opening months of Operation Barbarossa. The MiG-3, delivered during the second half of 1941, proved little better with a 1,350-hp (1007-kW) AM-35A engine, which gave the fighter a top speed of 398 mph (640 km/h); introduced at the same time was a constant-speed propeller, increased wing dihedral and improved cockpit canopy. Handling was only marginally improved, so the MiG-3 was transferred to attack bomber escort and close support duties. In 1942 two 12.7-mm

(0.5-in) machine-guns were added in underwing fairings by operational units, but gradually the aircraft was replaced by radial-engined fighters such as the La-5. Total production was said to be about 4,000, of which 2,100 were the earlier MiG-1.

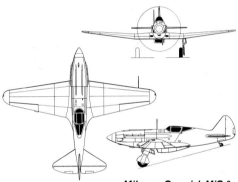

Mikoyan-Gurevich MiG-3

Specification: Mikoyan MiG-3
Type: single-seat fighter
Powerplant: one 1,350-hp (1007-kW) Mikulin AM-35A inline piston
Performance: max speed 398 mph (640 km/h) at 12,880 ft (3925 m); initial climb rate 3,935 ft (1200 m) per minute; service ceiling 39,370 ft (12000 m); range 777 miles (1250 km)
Weights: empty 5,996 lb (2720 kg); normal loaded 7,694 lb (3490 kg)
Dimensions: span 33 ft 9½ in (10.30 m); length 26 ft 9 in (8.15 m); height 8 ft 9 in (2.67 m); wing area 187.7 sq ft (17.44 m²)
Armament: one 12.7-mm (0.5-in) Beresin BS and two 7.62-mm (0.3-in) ShKAS nose guns (later plus two 12.7-mm/0.5-in underwing guns); six 82-mm (3.23-in) rockets or two 220-lb (100-kg) bombs

Introduced to overcome some of the tricky handling problems in the MiG-1, the MiG-3 was always regarded as an unforgiving aeroplane, and the increased power from its Mikulin AM-35A did nothing to alleviate a vicious torque-induced swing on take-off. These fighters in winter camouflage await delivery to front-line units.

Mitsubishi J2M 'Jack'

Unusual among Japanese fighters in combining a four-cannon armament with high rate of climb, the J2M Raiden ('Jack' to the Allies) was widely deployed for defence of the homeland against American bombing raids.

Although designed to a 1939 requirement, the **Mitsubishi J2M Raiden** (Thunderbolt) only came into its own while defending the Japanese homeland against American raids in the last year of the war. The Japanese navy's emphasis upon speed and climb rate, rather than its customary demands for range and manoeuvrability, prompted the designer Jiro Hirikoshi to adopt a squat single-engined design with long-chord radial engine cowling, laminar-flow wings and a highly raked, curved windscreen. First flight of the prototype **J2M1** took place on 20 March 1942, but the aircraft soon attracted criticism from navy pilots on numerous counts, not least that the view from the cockpit was inadequate. Modifications to rectify these shortcomings were delayed owing to Mitsubishi's preoccupation with the A6M. Production **J2M2**s left the factory slowly and entered service with the 381st Kokutai late in 1943, and were followed by the **J2M3** with a stronger wing stressed to mount four 20-mm cannon. The heavier armament restricted the performance of the Raiden to the extent that it no longer met the original demands, and the **J2M4** was an attempt to restore the per-

formance by including a turbocharger. The final production variant, the **J2M5** (34 built), was powered by a 1,820-hp (1358-kW) Mitsubishi Kasei 26a radial. In acknowledgement of the fact that J2Ms could not combat the B-29s at their operating altitudes, some J2M3s were armed with two upward-firing 20-mm cannon in addition to their wing guns.

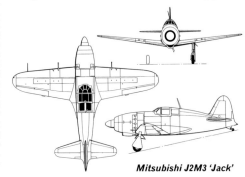

Mitsubishi J2M3 'Jack'

The first close look many Americans got of Japan was when they landed at this fighter base 32 miles (51 km) from Tokyo. The flotsam of a beaten air force was assembled at Atsugi Airfield, including these well-ventilated 'Jacks'. In all, a total of 476 Mitsubishi J2Ms were built.

Specification:
Mitsubishi J2M3 'Jack'
Type: single-seat fighter
Powerplant: one 1,800-hp (1343-kW) Mitsubishi Kasei 23a radial piston
Performance: max speed 365 mph (588 km/h) at 17,390 ft (5300 m); climb to 32,810 ft (10000 m) in 19.5 minutes; service ceiling 38,385 ft (11700 m); range 575 miles (925 km)
Weights: empty 5,423 lb (2460 kg); normal loaded 7,573 lb (3435 kg)
Dimensions: span 35 ft 5¼ in (10.80 m); length 32 ft 7½ in (9.95 m); height 12 ft 11½ in (3.95 m); wing area 215.82 sq ft (20.05 m²)
Armament: four wing-mounted 20-mm Type 99 cannon; some aircraft also armed with two upward-firing 20-mm cannon

Mitsubishi Ki-21 'Sally'

This Ki-21-IIb has a 12.7-mm (0.5-in) heavy machine-gun in a dorsal turret. Aircraft of this type were used on Japanese suicide commando-style attacks against American bases in the Pacific in the closing months of the war.

Although acknowledged by the Japanese as approaching obsolescence at the beginning of the Pacific war, the **Mitsubishi Ki-21** 'heavy' bomber (or, by British and American standards of the time, a light/medium bomber) remained in production until 1944 and was still in service one year later. Designed to a 1936 requirement, the first Ki-21 made its maiden flight on 18 December that year, and when the 60th and 61st Sentais arrived in China with their **Ki-21-Is** late in 1938 it could be said that the first stage in the Japanese army air force's modernisation programme had been completed. However, bearing in mind the lack of effective fighter opposition, the army authorities were aware that in the context of a war with the USA and UK the Ki-21 would be vulnerable to fighter attack and, late in 1939, Mitsubishi was instructed to improve the bomber's performance, with the result that by the beginning of the Pacific war the early 850-hp (634 kW) Ha-6 radials had been replaced by 1,500-hp (1119-kW) Ha-101 engines in much larger nacelles. The new version, the **Ki-21-II** (codenamed **'Sally'** by the Allies) was produced in two forms: the **Ki-21-IIa** retained the large 'green-house' with hand-held 7.7-mm (0.303-in) gun in the rear dorsal position, and the **Ki-21-IIb** had the 'greenhouse' replaced by a turret mounting a 12.7-mm (0.5-in) gun. Despite quickly accelerating losses to Allied fighters from 1942, Ki-21 units were operational almost to the end of the war.

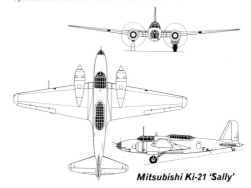

Mitsubishi Ki-21 'Sally'

Specification:
Mitsubishi Ki-21-IIb 'Sally'
Type: five-crew bomber
Powerplant: two 1,500-hp (1119-kW) Mitsubishi Ha-101 radial pistons
Performance: max speed 302 mph (486 km/h) at 15,485 ft (4720 m); climb to 19,685 ft (6000 m) in 13.2 minutes; service ceiling 32,810 ft (10000 m); range 1,680 miles (2700 km)
Weights: empty 13,382 lb (6070 kg); max take-off 23,391 lb (10610 kg)
Dimensions: span 73 ft 9¾ in (22.50 m); length 52 ft 5⅞ in (16.00 m); height 15 ft 10⅞ in (4.85 m); wing area 749.2 sq ft (69.60 m²)
Armament: 7.7-mm (0.303-in) Type 89 guns in nose, ventral, and beam positions, one 12.7-mm (0.5-in) Type 1 gun in dorsal turret; max bomb load 2,205 lb (1000 kg)

Originally codenamed 'Jane' by the Allies, after General MacArthur's wife (a compliment not appreciated), the Ki-21 was hurriedly renamed 'Sally'. A total of 777 Ki-21-Is and 1,278 Ki-21-IIs was built by Mitsubishi and Nakajima, employed by the Japanese throughout the Pacific war.

Mitsubishi A6M 'Zeke'

This A6M2 belonged to the 12th Combined Kokutai, Hankow region of China, in the winter of 1940-41. Total production of all A6Ms was 10,937. (The reporting name 'Zeke' was given to the A6M, and 'Rufe' to a float version, the A6M2-N.)

The **A6M 'Zero'** was the first carrierborne fighter capable of outperforming any contemporary land-based fighter it would confront. Designed under the leadership of Jiro Horikoshi in 1937 as a replacement for the A5M, the prototype **A6M1** was first flown on 1 April 1939 with a 780-hp (582-kW) Mitsubishi Zuisei 13 radial; production **A6M2**s with two wing-mounted 20-mm guns and two nose-mounted 7.7-mm (0.303-in) guns were fitted with the 950-hp (709-kW) Nakajima Sakae 12 radial, and it was with this version that the Japanese navy escorted the force sent against Pearl Harbor, and gained air superiority over Malaya, the Philippines and Burma. In 1942 the **A6M3** with two-stage supercharged Sakae 21 entered service, later aircraft having their folding wingtips removed. The Battle of Midway represented the Zero-Sen's combat zenith; thereafter, the agile Japanese fighter found itself ever more outclassed by the American F6F Hellcat and P-38 Lightning. To counter the new American fighters the **A6M5** was rushed to front-line units; this version, with Sakae 21 engine and improved exhaust system, possessed a top speed of 351 mph (565 km/h) and more A6M5s (and sub-variants) were produced than any other Japanese aircraft. Five A6M5s of the Shikishima *kamikaze* unit sank the carrier *St Lo* and damaged three others on 25 October 1944. Other versions were the **A6M6** with water-methanol boosted Sakae 31 engine, and the **A6M7** fighter/dive-bomber.

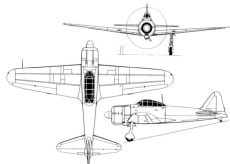

Mitsubishi A6M2 'Zeke'

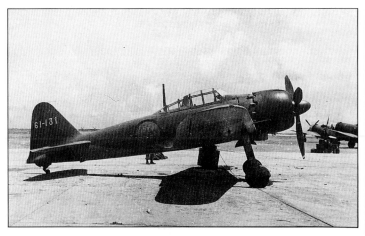

Fatally underestimated by the Allies at the outbreak of the Pacific war, the Zero-Sen ran circles round RAF Hurricane and Buffalo fighters in Malaya prior to the fall of Singapore. The late A6M5 version, seen here, was captured intact by the Americans in 1944.

Specification:
Mitsubishi A6M5b 'Zeke'
Type: single-seat fighter
Powerplant: one 1,100-hp (821-kW) Nakajima NK2F Sakae 21 radial piston
Performance: max speed 351 mph (565 km/h) at 19,685 ft (6000 m); climb to 19,685 ft (6000 m) in 7.0 minutes; service ceiling 38,520 ft (11740 m); range 710 (1143 km)
Weights: empty 4,136 lb (1876 kg); normal loaded 6,025 lb (2733 kg)
Dimensions: span 36 ft 1 in (11.00 m); length 29 ft 11⅛ in (9.12 m); height 11 ft 6⅛ in (3.51 m); wing area 229.27 sq ft (21.30 m²)
Armament: one 7.7-mm (0.303-in) Type 97 and one 13.2-mm (0.52-in) Type 3 machine-gun in nose, two wing-mounted 20-mm Type 99 cannon; two 132- or 551-lb (60- or 250-kg) bombs

Mitsubishi G4M 'Betty'

Identified by its dihedral tailplane, the Mitsubishi G4M3 was produced in limited numbers during the last two years of the war. Portrayed here is an aircraft of the Yokosuka Kokutai, Atsugi, as it appeared in September 1945.

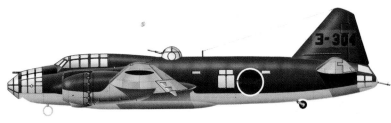

Codenamed **'Betty'** by the Allies, the **Mitsubishi G4M** long-range medium bomber remained in service with the Japanese navy from the first to the last day of the war; it took part in the attack that sank the British warships HMS *Prince of Wales* and HMS *Repulse* in December 1941 – and carried the Japanese surrender delegation on 19 August 1945. Designed to a 1937 requirement for a long-range bomber, the **G4M1** prototype made its first flight on 23 October 1939, and during trials recorded an extraordinary performance of 276 mph (444 km/h) top speed and 3,450 mile (5555 km) range, albeit without bomb load. The first production G4M1s were initially deployed against China in mid-1941 but on the eve of the attack on Malaya the bombers moved to Indo-China and within a week had successfully attacked the *Prince of Wales* and *Repulse*. When Allied fighter opposition eventually increased to effective proportions, the G4M1 was seen to be very vulnerable, possessing little armour protection for crew and fuel tanks, and it was in a pair of G4M1s that Admiral Yamamoto and his staff were travelling when shot down by P-38s over Bougainville on 18 April 1943. The

G4M2 was therefore introduced with increased armament, increased fuel and 1,800-hp (1343-kW) Mitsubishi Kasei radials, and this version remained in production until the end of the war. A further improved version, the **G4M3**, with increased crew protection, was also produced in small numbers.

Mitsubishi G4M 'Betty'

Specification:
Mitsubishi G4M2 'Betty'
Type: seven-crew land-based naval bomber
Powerplant: two 1,800-hp (1343-kW) Mitsubishi MK4P Kasei 21 radial pistons
Performance: max speed 272 mph (438 km/h) at 15,090 ft (4600 m); climb to 26,245 ft (8000 m) in 32.4 minutes; ceiling 29,365 ft (8950 m); range 3,765 miles (6059 km)
Weights: empty 17,990 lb (8160 kg); normal loaded 27,558 lb (12500 kg)
Dimensions: span 82 ft 0¼ in (25.00 m); length 67 ft 7⅞ in (20.00 m); height 19 ft 8 in (6.00 m); wing area 840.93 sq ft (78.125 m²)
Armament: two 7.7-mm (0.303-in) Type 92 guns in nose & one in side positions, one dorsal 20-mm Type 99 cannon & one in tail; 2,205 lb (1000 kg) of bombs or one 1,764-lb (800-kg) torpedo

The Mitsubishi G4M came to be widely used in the Pacific war from beginning to end. This example, believed to be a G4M2e, is seen carrying an Ohka suicide bomb, a version that saw action during the last six months of the war. Production amounted to 1,200 G4M1s, 1,154 G4M2s and 60 G4M3s.

Mitsubishi Ki-46 'Dinah'

The excellent Ki-46-III entered service late in 1943, delivery priority being given to war fronts where the Allies had gained air superiority. Shown is an aircraft of the 19th Dokuritsu Dai Shijugo Chutai, which was based in Japan at the end of the war.

The **Ki-46** two-seat reconnaissance aircraft was designed during 1938 under the direction of Tomio Kubo, who produced a twin-engined low-wing monoplane with slim fuselage and straight-tapered wings and tail surfaces. When first flown in November 1939, the prototype Ki-46, powered by Ha-26-I engines of only 900 hp (670 kW), returned a speed of 335 mph (529 km/h), faster than the navy's new Zero-Sen fighter. With the adoption of two-stage supercharged Ha-102 radials of 1,080 hp (806 kW), the production **Ki-46-II**, which began coming off the line in March 1941, was capable of a speed of 375 mph (604 km/h), then well beyond any Allied fighter. A Ki-46-II was flown on clandestine sorties without interference over Malaya before the outbreak of war to reconnoitre the proposed invasion areas. Many months later, in anticipation of the arrival of Spitfire Mk Vs and P-38s in the Pacific theatre, the **Ki-46-III** (code-named **'Dinah'** by the Allies) was introduced with improved nose shape, fuel injection and revised exhaust system to give some thrust augmentation, these modifications increasing the top speed to 391 mph (630 km/h). Operating at heights over 30,000 ft (9145 m), the aircraft maintained a watch for B-29s in the Marianas, but eventually suffered mounting losses with the arrival of the P-47N fighter from the USA. Not as adaptable as the British Mosquito or American P-38, the Ki-46 was one of the best reconnaissance aircraft of the Pacific war.

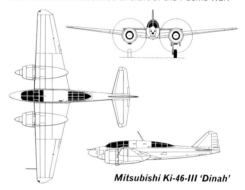

Mitsubishi Ki-46-III 'Dinah'

Codenamed 'Dinah' by the Allies, the Ki-46 was an attractive aircraft which was widely used by the Japanese in numerous roles, including that of night-fighter. This is a Ki-46-II with nose cannon and an upward-firing cannon. Production of the Ki-46-II reached 1,093, and that of the Ki-46-III 609.

Specification:
Mitsubishi Ki-46-III 'Dinah'
Type: two-seat reconnaissance aircraft
Powerplant: two 1,500-hp (1119-kW) Mitsubishi Ha-112-II radials
Performance: max speed 391 mph (630 km/h) at 19,685 ft (6000 m); climb to 26,250 ft (8000 m) in 20.25 minutes; service ceiling 34,450 ft (10500 m); range 2,485 miles (4000 km)
Weights: empty 8,446 lb (3831 kg); max take-off 14,330 lb (6500 kg)
Dimensions: span 48 ft 2¼ in (14.70 m); length 36 ft 1 in (11.00 m); height 12 ft 8¾ in (3.88 m); wing area 344.44 sq ft (32.00 m²)
Armament: two 20-mm Ho-5 forward-firing cannon in nose

Mitsubishi Ki-67 'Peggy'

The Mitsubishi Ki-67 was ordered into mass production at Mitsubishi, Kawasaki and Tachikawa, but only a total of 698 examples was eventually built. Some aircraft flew in kamikaze strikes.

Like the Ki-21 and G4M, the **Ki-67 Hirya** (Flying Dragon) was classified by the Japanese as a heavy bomber, yet by Western standards it would have scarcely rated the medium bomber category. It was nevertheless the best bomber to serve Japan in the war, albeit too late to influence the tide of events of the last year. By then, the American air raids on the Japanese homeland were devastating aircraft plants and production was seriously affected. The Ki-67 was designed to a 1940 specification for a strategic bomber intended for use in an anticipated war with the Soviet Union on the Siberia-Manchukuo border. Design of the prototype Ki-67 was protracted by departing from established Japanese practice and including armour protection and self-sealing fuel tanks, and it was not until 27 December 1942 that the first aircraft flew; it proved to be highly manoeuvrable and pleasant to fly, and possessed a top speed of 334 mph (538 km/h). In the same month it was decided to adapt some Ki-67s as torpedo-bombers. The army put forward such a host of suggestions for additional equipment that production suffered long delays, and it was not until October 1944 that the Ki-67

(codenamed **'Peggy'** by the Allies) was first flown in combat by the 7th and 98th Sentais, and by the navy's 762nd Kokutai in the torpedo role during the battle off Formosa. Modifications were held to a minimum as production was afforded the highest priority, but American B-29 raids (and an earthquake in December 1944) disrupted production.

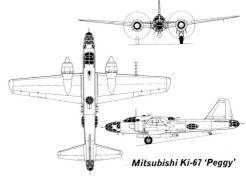

Mitsubishi Ki-67 'Peggy'

Specification:
Mitsubishi Ki-67 'Peggy'
Type: six/eight-crew bomber
Powerplant: two 1,900-hp (1417-kW) Mitsubishi Ha-104 radial pistons
Performance: max speed 334 mph (537 km/h) at 19,980 ft (6090 m); climb to 19,685 ft (6000 m) in 14.5 minutes; ceiling 31,070 ft (9470 m); range 1,740 miles (2800 km)
Weights: empty 19,068 lb (8649 kg); normal loaded 30,347 lb (13765 kg)
Dimensions: span 73 ft 9¾ in (22.50 m); length 61 ft 4¼ in (18.70 m); height 25 ft 3⅛ in (7.70 m); wing area 708.8 sq ft (65.85 m²)
Armament: 12.7-mm (0.5-in) Type 1 guns in nose, beam positions & tail, one dorsal 20-mm He-5 cannon; 1,764 lb (800 kg) bombs, or one 2,359-lb (1070-kg) torpedo, or (*kamikaze* mission) 6,393 lb (2900 kg) bombs

Although classified as a heavy bomber (by Japanese standards), the Ki-67 was closer to the American B-26 Marauder medium bomber in concept. It was probably the best of all army and navy bombers but arrived in service too late to influence the Pacific war. This Ki-67-Ib belonged to the 98th Sentai, 3rd Chutai.

Morane-Saulnier MS.406

Outdated in 1940 and outclassed by the modern Luftwaffe aircraft in the Battle of France, the MS.406 equipped 14 groupes de chasse at the time of the German attack on 10 May. The aircraft shown here carries the stork emblem of GC I/2, based at Toul/Ochey.

Most numerous of French fighters at the time of Germany's attack in the west in 1940, the **MS.406** was ordered into production in 1937 when its performance was already notably far below that of current British and German fighters. Moreover, its complicated development within the MS.405-411 family was as wasteful of effort as it was counterproductive. The prototype MS.406 was in fact the fourth development MS.405 and first flew on 20 May 1938 with 860-hp (642-kW) Hispano-Suiza 12Y 31 and *moteur-canon*, typifying the continental practice of using a hub-firing cannon to avoid the need to synchronise its fire. By April 1938 orders totalling 955 MS.406s had been placed, for completion by September 1939, but in the event only 572 had been produced by that date. At the outbreak of war these aircraft equipped five *groupes de chasse* at Chartres and Dijon, plus two in Algeria; 29 aircraft had been shipped to Tunisia and 10 to Indo-China. By 10 May 1940 the number of combat-ready MS.406s had actually dropped from 367 to 278, a situation quickly aggravated by the loss of 37 aircraft on the ground at Cambrai, Damblain, Vitry and Le Quesnoy on the first day.

The MS.406 rapidly proved to be outclassed in the air, and during the Battle of France 150 were lost in combat (plus 100 on the ground). The aircraft's inferiority was acknowledged and, by the time of the armistice, conversion to other aircraft was already being undertaken by 10 MS.406 *groupes*.

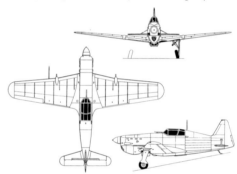

Morane-Saulnier MS.406C-1

An early example of the cantilever monoplane fighter, the MS.406 was underpowered and retained such obsolescent features as a braced tailplane and a measure of fabric covering. This formation is pictured over the French Front in 1939/40.

Specification:
Morane-Saulnier MS.406
Type: single-seat fighter
Powerplant: one 860-hp (642-kW) Hispano-Suiza HS 12Y 31 inline piston
Performance: max speed 304 mph (490 km/h) at 14,765 ft (4500 m); climb to 19,685 ft (6000 m) in 9.0 minutes; service ceiling 32,810 ft (10000 m); range 684 miles (1100 km)
Weights: empty 4,178 lb (1895 kg); normal loaded 5,600 lb (2540 kg)
Dimensions: span 34 ft 9½ in (10.62 m); length 26 ft 9⅓ m (8.17 m); height 10 ft 8⅓ in (3.25 m); wing area 172.2 sq ft (16.00 m²)
Armament: one 20-mm HS 404 hub-firing cannon and two 7.5-mm (0.295-in) MAC 1934 machine-guns in wings

Nakajima B5N 'Kate'

As the most modern naval attack aircraft then in service, the B5N delivered the attack at Pearl Harbor, carrying torpedoes specially adapted to run in shallow waters. The aircraft shown here is equipped with torpedo crutches.

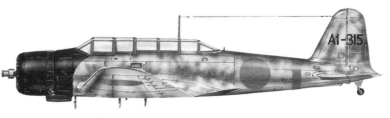

Designed to a 1935 requirement, and already in service for four years when Japan entered the war, the **Nakajima B5N 'Kate'** in 1941 was without question the best carrierborne torpedo-bomber in the world. Powered by a Nakajima Hikari radial engine, the low-wing three-crew monoplane with inwards-retracting, wide-track landing gear was exceptionally clean, and first flew in January 1937. The following year production **B5N1**s were embarking in Japan's carriers as shore-based units were deployed in China. In 1939 the improved **B5N2** appeared with a more powerful Sakae 11 engine in a smaller cowling, although armament and bomb load remained unchanged. When Japan attacked the USA the B5N2 had wholly replaced the B5N1 with operational units, and 144 B5N2s were involved in the fateful attack on Pearl Harbor; within the next 12 months aircraft of this type sank the American carriers USS *Hornet*, USS *Lexington* and USS *Yorktown*. The B5N certainly earned the respect of the Americans, and in all the major carrier battles of the Pacific war attracted the undivided attention of defending fighters. With its defensive armament of one machine-gun and laden with a large bomb or torpedo, however, the B5N began to suffer heavily, and although they were committed during the Solomons campaign the survivors were withdrawn from combat after the 1944 Philippine battles. Due to their excellent range, they were assigned to anti-submarine and maritime reconnaissance duties beyond the range of Allied fighters.

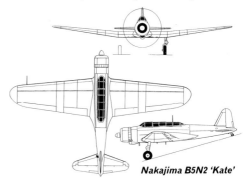

Nakajima B5N2 'Kate'

Specification:
Nakajima B5N2 'Kate'
Type: three-crew carrierborne torpedo-bomber
Powerplant: one 1,000-hp (746-kW) Nakajima NK1B Sakae 11 radial piston
Performance: max speed 235 mph (378 km/h) at 11,810 ft (3600 m); climb to 9,845 ft (3000 m) in 7.7 minutes; service ceiling 27,100 ft (8260 m); range 1,237 miles (1990 km)
Weights: empty 5,024 lb (2279 kg); max take-off 9,039 lb (4100 kg)
Dimensions: span 50 ft 10⅞ in (15.52 m); length 33 ft 9½ in (10.30 m); height 12 ft 1⅝ in (3.70 m); wing area 405.8 sq ft (37.70 m²)
Armament: one 7.7-mm (0.303-in) Type 92 flexible machine-gun in rear cockpit; one 1,764-lb (800-kg) torpedo or equivalent weight of bombs

A pair of Sakae-powered B5N2s flies over ships of the Imperial Japanese navy. Codenamed 'Kate' by the Allies, this was the version that delivered the fatal blows against the American carriers USS **Hornet**, **Lexington** *and* **Yorktown** *in 1942. Production of all B5Ns reached 1,149.*

Nakajima B6N 'Jill'

This B6N2 is of the type that entered service in the last 18 months of the war, after American fighters had gained almost universal air superiority. Codenamed 'Jill', they were used for kamikaze attacks during the Okinawa campaign.

At a time when the triumphs of the B5N were still almost three years in the future, the Japanese navy issued a specification for a replacement, recognising that only limited overall design improvement of the B5N could be achieved in the B5N2. Accordingly. design went ahead in 1939 of the **B6N Tenzan** (Heavenly Mountain) and, despite the navy's preference for the Mitsubishi Kasei radial, a Nakajima Mamoru was selected for the prototype which flew early in 1941. Superficially, the B6N resembled the earlier aircraft, but the much increased power and torque of the big engine and four-bladed propeller was found to impose considerable directional stability problems, demanding that the vertical tail surfaces be offset to one side. Flight trials dragged on and were further delayed by troubles during carrier acceptance tests, then Nakajima was ordered to stop production of the Mamoru engine and modifications had to be introduced for the Kasei. **B6N1**s were embarked in the carriers *Shokaku, Taiho, Hiyo, Junyo* and *Zuikaku*, and took part in the great Battle of the Philippine Sea of June 1943, many being lost when the three first-named carriers were sunk. In that month pro-

duction started of the slightly improved **B6N2** (of which 1,133 were produced before the end of the war), but the heavy losses among Japanese carriers resulted in the 'Jill' being largely deployed ashore, particularly after the Battle of Leyte Gulf.

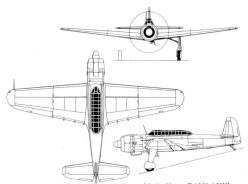

Nakajima B6N2 'Jill'

Early Nakajima B6N1 Tenzans (of which only 133 were built) were fitted with a Mamoru 11 radial of 1,870 hp (1394 kW). When production of this engine was prematurely suspended, Nakajima opted to switch to the 1,850-hp (1379-kW) Mitsubishi Kasei 25. 'Jills' were used extensively in the last two years of the war.

Specification: Nakajima B6N2 'Jill'
Type: three-crew carrierborne torpedo-bomber
Powerplant: one 1,850-hp (1380-kW) Mitsubishi MK4T Kasei 25 radial piston
Performance: max speed 299 mph (481 km/h) at 16,075 ft (4900 m); climb to 16,405 ft (5000 m) in 10.4 minutes; ceiling 29,660 ft (9040 m); range 1,085 miles (1746 km)
Weights: empty 6,636 Lb (3010 kg); max take-off 12,456 Lb (5650 kg)
Dimensions: span 48 ft 10⅜ in (14.89 m); length 35 ft 7½ in (10.87 m); height 12 ft 5⅛ in (3.80 m); wing area 400.42 sq ft (37.20 m²)
Armament: one flexible 13-mm (0.51-in) Type 2 machine-gun in rear cockpit and one 7.7-mm (0.303-in) Type 97 gun in ventral tunnel; one 1,764-lb (800-kg) torpedo or equivalent weight of bombs

Nakajima Ki-43 'Oscar'

A Ki-43-IIa of the 2nd Chutai, 25th Fighter Sentai, a unit that fought in China during 1944 and until about March 1945. First flown early in 1939, it was outclassed by American fighters by the last two years of the war.

With its relatively low-powered radial engine, two-bladed propeller and twin rifle-calibre machine-gun armament, the **Ki-43 Hayabusa** (Peregrine Falcon) was the most dangerously underestimated Japanese fighter of the early months of the Pacific war; flown by Japanese army air force pilots, it gained complete mastery over Brewster Buffaloes and Hawker Hurricanes in Burma. It resulted from a 1937 design which emerged as a lightweight fighter-bomber that required no more than 950 hp (709 kW) to meet its speed demands. In common with other Japanese fighters of the time, its armament was puny by RAF standards, and the aircraft possessed neither armour nor self-sealing fuel tanks. As the Allied air forces pulled themselves together after the first shock of defeat, the Ki-43's weaknesses were discovered and losses mounted, resulting in the introduction of the Ki-43 (**'Oscar'** to the Allies), with pilot armour, rudimentary self-sealing fuel tanks and reflector gunsight; the engine was also changed to the 1,150-hp (858-kW) Nakajima Ha-115 radial which increased the top speed to 329 mph (530 km/h), roughly the same as that of the

Hurricane Mk I. The **Ki-43-IIb** entered mass production in November 1942, first with Nakajima and six months later with Tachikawa. Final variant was the **Ki-43-III** with 1,230-hp (918-kW) engine and a top speed of 358 mph (576 km/h), but relatively few examples reached operational units.

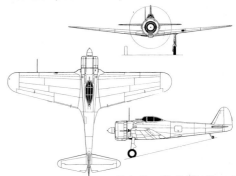

Nakajima Ki-43-I-Ko 'Oscar'

Specification:
Nakajima Ki-43-IIb 'Oscar'
Type: single-seat fighter-bomber
Powerplant: one 1,150-hp (858-kW) Nakajima Ha-115 radial piston
Performance: max speed 329 mph (530 km/h) at 13,125 ft (4000 m); climb to 16,405 ft (5000 m) in 5.8 minutes; service ceiling 36,750 ft (11200 m); range 1,095 miles (1760 km)
Weights: empty 4,211 lb (1910 kg); max take-off 6,450 lb (2925 kg)
Dimensions: span 35 ft 6¼ in (10.84 m); length 29 ft 3⅜ in (8.92 m); height 10 ft 8¾ in (3.27 m); wing area 230.37 sq ft (21.40 m²)
Armament: two 12.7-mm (0.5-in) Ho 103 machine-guns in wings; two 250-kg (551-lb) bombs under wings

The Ki-43-IIb (seen here) differed from the IIa by having repositioned wing hardpoints, as earlier aircraft had lost their propellers when dropping bombs. The Hayabusa was available in such large numbers (production totalled 5,886, plus 33 prototypes) that it continued to be widely deployed right up to the end of the war.

Nakajima Ki-49 'Helen'

This example of the up-engined and more heavily armed Ki-49-II served with the 3rd Chutai, 62nd Sentai, in Burma, the Dutch East Indies and New Guinea during 1944. The type was codenamed 'Helen' by the Allies.

The **Ki-49 Donryu** (Storm Dragon) was intended to replace the Ki-21, and although it included modern design features it proved a disappointment in service, representing a great deal of aeroplane to carry a crew of eight and a maximum bomb load of only 2,205 Lb (1000 kg) over a sortie radius of 500 miles (800 km). Design began in 1938 and the first prototype made its maiden flight in August 1939 with a pair of 1,080-hp (806-kW) Ha-5 radials. Production **Ki-49-I** bombers started delivery to the Japanese army air force in August 1941 and by the end of the year the 61st Sentai was partially equipped. The Ki-49-I was first flown on operations over China, and later over New Guinea, taking part in a number of raids over Australia's Northern Territory. The Ki-49 was unusual among early Japanese bombers in including armour protection for the crew and self-sealing fuel tanks. Despite a top speed of 300 mph (483 km/h), and well-distributed gun armament, it proved very vulnerable to Allied fighters and losses mounted quickly from mid-1942. In the **Ki-49-II**, which entered service in late 1942, most of the 7.7-mm (0.303-in) guns were replaced by 12.7-mm (0.5-in) weapons, and

the 1,250-hp (933-kW) Ha-41 radials gave place to 1,500-hp (1119-kW) Ha-109s. This, the major production version, never wholly replaced the Ki-21, and in the last year of the war Ki-49-IIs were diverted for use as night-fighters, as transports and in suicide attacks at Mindoro in December 1944.

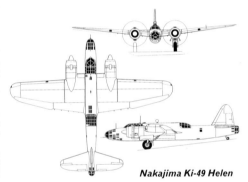

Nakajima Ki-49 Helen

The Ki-49 Donryu was just starting delivery to the Japanese army air force when the Pacific war started. The early Ki-49-I was criticised by service crews as being tricky to handle and possessing a disappointing performance. Production totalled 23 prototypes and 796 production examples.

Specification: Nakajima Ki-49-IIa 'Helen'
Type: eight-crew heavy bomber
Powerplant: two 1,500-hp (1119-kW) Nakajima Ha-109 radial pistons
Performance: max speed 306 mph (492 km/h) at 16,405 ft (5000 m); climb to 16,405 ft (5000 m) in 13.6 minutes; ceiling 30,510 ft (9300 m); range 1,243 miles (2000 km)
Weights: empty 14,396 lb (6530 kg); max take-off 25,133 lb (11400 kg)
Dimensions: span 67 ft 0⅛ in (2.042 m); length 54 ft 1½ in (16.50 m); height 13 ft 11¼ in (4.25 m); wing area 743.25 sq ft (69.05 m²)
Armament: (Ki-49-IIb) 12.7-mm (0.5-in) Ho-103 machine-guns in nose, ventral and tail positions, two beam 7.7-mm (0.303-in) Type 89 guns, one dorsal 20-mm Ho-1 cannon; 2,205 lb (1000 kg) bombs

Nakajima Ki-84 'Frank'

Bearing the blue spinner and tail markings of the 1st Chutai, 47th Sentai, this Ki-84-I was based at Narumatsu, Japan, for home defence in 1945. Such late production aircraft matched the performance of American fighters.

Best of all Japanese fighters available in quantity during the last year of the war, the **Ki-84 Hayate** (Gale) not only possessed a reasonable performance but, unusual among Japanese aircraft, carried a powerful armament capable of knocking down the heavily armed and armoured American bombers. Not flown in prototype form until April 1943, the Ki-84 met with immediate approval by Japanese army air force pilots, but was subjected to lengthy service trials which undoubtedly delayed its introduction to combat operations. Production got underway at Nakajima's Ota plant in April 1944, pre-production aircraft having equipped the 22nd Sentai in China the previous month. Immediately afterwards, 10 Sentais of the Ki-84-I, codenamed **'Frank'** by the Allies, were deployed in the Philippines to confront the advancing American forces. In an effort to accelerate production of the excellent new fighter, Nakajima opened up a new line at its Otsonomiya plant, and as the American B-29 raids began to take their toll on Japanese cities a new 'bomber destroyer', the **Ki-84-Ic**, was produced with an armament of two nose-mounted 20-mm cannon and two wing-mounted 30-mm can-

non. Some measure of the importance attached to the Ki-84 is that in the last 17 months of war 3,382 aircraft were built, this despite the tremendous havoc wrought by the B-29 raids and the fact that, owing to such damage at Musashi, Nakajima's engine plant had to be transferred elsewhere.

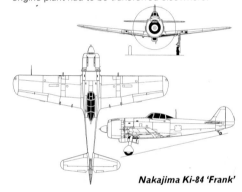

Nakajima Ki-84 'Frank'

Specification:
Nakajima Ki-84-Ia 'Frank'
Type: single-seat fighter and fighter-bomber
Powerplant: one 1,800-hp (1343-kW) Nakajima Ha-45 radial piston
Performance: max speed 392 mph (631 km/h) at 20,080 ft (6120 m); climb to 16,405 ft (5000 ft) in 5.9 minutes; service ceiling 34,450 ft (10500 m); range 1,053 miles (1695 km)
Weights: empty 5,864 Lb (2660 kg); max take-off 8,576 Lb (3890 kg)
Dimensions: span 36 ft 10½ in (11.24 m); length 32 ft 6¼ in (9.92 m); height 11 ft 1¼ in (3.39 m); wing area 226.04 sq ft (21.00 m²)
Armament: two nose-mounted 12.7-mm (0.5-in) Ho-103 machine-guns and two wing-mounted 20-mm Ho-5 cannon; two 250-kg (551-lb) bombs under wings

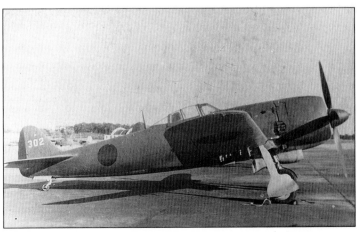

Had it been available earlier and in large numbers, the excellent Hayate might have posed problems for the Allies, for it had a higher rate of climb and better manoeuvrability than the P-51H or P-47N operating in the Pacific zone. American pilots spoke highly of these aircraft when they were evaluated in the USA.

North American B-25 Mitchell

The Mitchell served with numerous Allied air forces during the war, and this 12-gun aircraft is shown in the markings of the Royal Australian Air Force. The majority of B-25Js flew in the south-west Pacific theatre.

Initially flown on 19 August 1940, the first B-25 was completed with full-wing dihedral but inadequate directional stability led to a reduction of dihedral outboard of the engines in later aircraft, producing the gull-wing appearance that was to characterise the Mitchell. **B-25A**s started arriving with the 17th Bomb Group in 1941, and were followed by 120 **B-25B**s with increased gun armament, this version joining the RAF as the **Mitchell Mk I**. It was also B-25Bs that, led by Lieutenant Colonel James H. Doolittle, made the famous raid on Tokyo, having taken off from the carrier *Hornet* in April 1942. The **B-26C** and **B-26D** versions with much increased all-up weight and extra fuel capacity were produced at Inglewood, California (1,619 built), and at Dallas, Texas (2,290 built), respectively. The **B-25G** introduced the standard US Army nose-mounted 75-mm field gun, and 405 aircraft were produced. The version was inferior to the **B-25H**, which featured the lighter T-13E1 75-mm gun as well as no fewer than 14 0.5-in (12.7-mm) machine-guns. A return to the previous 'bomber' nose was made in the most-produced **B-25J** version, although it retained the four 'package' guns on the sides of the fuselage. In the final months of the war, when B-25Js flew low-level raids with diminishing fighter opposition, the bomb-aimer was discarded and eight machine-guns were mounted in a 'solid' nose, in addition to eight 5-in (127-mm) rocket projectiles under the wings.

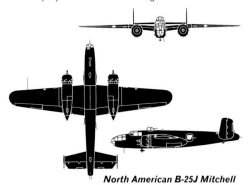

North American B-25J Mitchell

Famous for its brilliant raid on Tokyo led by Lieutenant Colonel Jimmie Doolittle in 1942, the B-25 light bomber was a sound design, well liked by its crews. The B-25D seen here was built at a North American factory at Kansas City. About 11,000 B-25s were built, of which the USAAF received 9,816 and the RAF 700.

Specification: North American B-25J Mitchell
Type: six-crew medium/light bomber
Powerplant: two 1,700-hp (1268-kW) Wright R-2600-92 radial pistons
Performance: max speed 272 mph (438 km/h) at 13,000 ft (3960 m); climb to 15,000 ft (4570 m) in 17.5 minutes; ceiling 24,200 ft (7375 m); range 1,350 miles (2173 km)
Weights: empty 19,480 Lb (8836 kg); max take-off 35,000 Lb (15876 kg)
Dimensions: span 67 ft 7 in (20.60 m); length 52 ft 11 in (16.13 m); height 16 ft 4 in (4.98 m); wing area 610.0 sq ft (56.67 m²)
Armament: 12 0.5-in (12.7 mm) machine-guns in extreme nose, sides of fuselage, dorsal turret, each beam position and tail; eight 5-in (127-mm) rockets under wing and 3,000-lb (136-kg) bomb load

North American P-51 Mustang

This Mustang Mk III is from No. 19 (Fighter) Sqn, RAF, based at Ford at the time of the great Normandy landings of June 1944. Many RAF Mustangs were fitted with a bulged sliding canopy, known as the Malcolm hood.

The **P-51 Mustang** was designed in 1940 to a British specification, the prototype NA-73 flying in October with a 1,100-hp (820-kW) Allison V-1710-F3F. Although two early aircraft were evaluated by the USAAF as **XP-51s**, the type was not adopted. Most of the early aircraft were supplied to the RAF (620 as **Mustang Mk 1As** and **Mk IIs**), but their poor performance prevented their use as fighters, relegating them instead to use in the ground support (army co-operation) role. After the USA's entry into the war the USAAF ordered 148 P-51s, which entered service with wing bomb shackles in the attack category as the **A-36A**. The British had re-engined four Mustangs with Rolls-Royce Merlins, transforming the aircraft, while in America the armament was reduced to four 0.5-in (12.7-mm) guns. A 1,200-hp (895-kW) Allison V-1710-81 was used in the **P-51A**, 310 being ordered in 1942. So spectacular were the benefits of the Merlin that a Packard-built Merlin (as the V-1650) was used in the **P-51B**, of which 1,988 were produced at Inglewood; 1,750 of the similar **P-51C** were built at Dallas. Later aircraft had the six-gun armament, while increased fuel capacity extended the range to 2,080 miles (3347 km). The **P-51D** featured a cut-down rear fuselage and 'tear drop' canopy. The Merlin P-51 joined the RAF as the **Mustang Mk III** (P-51B and P-51C) and **Mk IV** (P-51D). Fastest of all versions was the lightened **P-51H** with a top speed of 487 mph (784 km/h), 555 being built during the war.

North American P-51D (Mustang Mk IV)

Specification: North American P-51D (Mustang Mk IV)
Type: single-seat fighter
Powerplant: one 1,490-hp (1112-kW) Packard Rolls-Royce Merlin V-1650-7 inline piston
Performance: max speed 437 mph (704 km/h) at 25,000 ft (7620 m); climb to 30,000 ft (9145 m) in 13.0 minutes; service ceiling 41,900 ft (12770 m); max range 2,080 miles (3347 km)
Weights: empty 7,125 lb (3232 kg); max take-off 11,600 lb (5262 kg)
Dimensions: span 37 ft 0¼ in (11.28 m); length 32 ft 3¼ in (9.85 m); height 12 ft 2 in (3.71 m); wing area 233.2 sq ft (21.65 m²)
Armament: six 0.5-in (12.7-mm) machine-guns in wings; two 1,000-lb (454-kg) bombs or six 5-in (127-mm) rocket projectiles

This P-51K (also designated Mustang Mk IV) belonged to the Royal Air Force. The variant was generally similar to the P-51D and some 1,500 were produced, 594 being allocated to the RAF. Total production of all P-51s was 15,586, including 7,956 P-51Ds.

Northrop P-61 Black Widow

This P-61A-5 – 42-4464 'Jukin Judy' – belonged to the 422nd Night Fighter Squadron, based at Scorton. The aircraft wears the overall high-gloss black finish that dates from late 1944.

Despite the advances made by the night bomber since the earliest years of military aviation, the concept of a specialist night-fighter was almost universally ignored until 1940, and nowhere more so than in the United States. Spurred by events in Europe and encouraged by early British experiments with airborne radar, the US Army accepted proposals by Northrop in 1940 for a large twin-engined twin-boom night-fighter. The prototype of this, the **XP-61**, flew for the first time on 21 May 1942 and was named **Black Widow**. Thirteen **YP-61**s were followed by 200 production **P-61A**s. Armed with four 20-mm cannon under the nose and four 0.5-in (12.7-mm) machine-guns in a remotely-controlled dorsal turret (the latter omitted after the first 37 aircraft), the type obtained its first 'kill' with the 18th Fighter Group in the Pacific theatre on 7 July 1944. The **P-61B** – strictly speaking a night intruder – began to enter service that month, capable of carrying four 1,600-Lb (726-kg) bombs, and the final 250 aircraft of the order for 400 had the four-gun turret reinstated. This version was in service with the USAAF night-fighter squadrons in Europe in August 1944. Final wartime version was the **P-61C** (41 produced), powered by two 2,800-hp (2090-kW) R-2800-73s. The Black Widow proved a devastating weapon in the Far East during the last year of the war, and several squadrons were deployed in India and China for the defence of the newly-created B-29 bases.

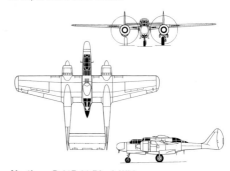

Northrop P-61B-20 Black Widow

The big Black Widow was the USAAF's first purpose-designed, radar-equipped night-fighter and entered service in mid-1944. This P-61A was one of the early aircraft, and featured AI radar developed from British equipment by the Massachusetts Institute of Technology.

Specification: Northrop P-61B Black Widow
Type: three-crew night-fighter/intruder
Powerplant: two 2,000-hp (1492-kW) Pratt & Whitney R-2800-65 radial pistons
Performance: max speed 366 mph (589 km/h) at 20,000 ft (6095 m); climb to 20,000 ft (6095 m) in 12.0 minutes; ceiling 33,100 ft (10090 m); range 1,590 miles (2559 km)
Weights: empty 22,000 lb (9980 kg); max take-off 38,000 lb (17240 kg)
Dimensions: span 66 ft 0 in (20.12 m); length 49 ft 7 in (15.11 m); height 14 ft 8 in (4.46 m); wing area 664.0 sq ft (61.69 m²)
Armament: four 20-mm cannon under nose and four 0.5-in (12.7-mm) guns in remotely-controlled dorsal turret; four 1,600-lb (726-kg) bombs or eight 5-in (127-mm) rockets under wings

Petlyakov Pe-2

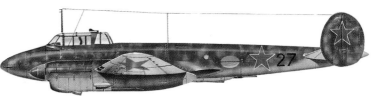

Often referred to as the 'Russian Mosquito', the Pe-2 was a versatile combat aircraft, the interceptor fighter version having a maximum speed of 408 mph (657 km/h). The bomber could carry up to 6,600 lb (2990 kg) of bombs.

Regarded with some disdain by ill-informed Western observers during the war, the **Petlyakov Pe-2** was superior to such aircraft as the Blenheim, Boston and Ventura. Designed by Vladimir Petlyakov's bureau, the prototype **VI-100** was powered by two Klimov inline engines (developed from Hispano-Suiza designs) and flew in 1939 as a high-altitude heavy fighter. Successful negotiation of its state trials in January 1940 was followed by production of the Pe-2 in June that year, the aircraft being adapted as a shallow-dive-attack bomber with dive-brakes added under the wings. With its top speed of 336 mph (540 km/h) it proved a fairly difficult adversary for the German fighters of 1941 but, with the advent of the Bf 109G, casualties began to increase, and in 1943, as production was rapidly extended in the Soviet Union, new versions with the 1,260-hp (940-kW) M-105PF engine, increased armament, additional armour and self-sealing fuel tanks appeared. With a top speed of 360 mph (580 km/h), this represented an effective battlefield support aircraft. Numerous air regiments were flying the Pe-2 as an attack bomber, the **Pe-21** heavy fighter, the **Pe-2R** long-range reconnais-sance aircraft, and the **Pe-3bis** reconnaissance fighter; final production versions were powered by 1,600-hp (1194-kW) M-107A engines which bestowed a top speed of 408 mph (657 km/h). A dual-control trainer, the **Pe-2U**, was also produced in the mid-war years.

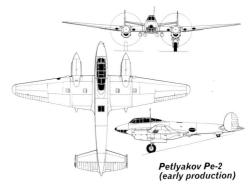

Petlyakov Pe-2 (early production)

Specification: Petlyakov Pe-2
Type: three-crew bomber
Powerplant: two 1,260-hp (940-kW) M-105PF inline pistons
Performance: max speed 360 mph (580 km/h) at 9,845 ft (3000 m); initial climb rate 1,410 ft (430 m) per minute; service ceiling 28,870 ft (8800 m); range 721 miles (1160 km)
Weights: empty 12,952 lb (5875 kg); max take-off 18,728 lb (8495 kg)
Dimensions: span 56 ft 3½ in (17.16 m); length 41 ft 6½ in (12.66 m); height 11 ft 6 in (3.50 m); wing area 436.0 sq ft (40.5 m²)
Armament: two fixed forward-firing 12.7-mm (0.5-in) UBS guns, one each dorsal and ventral 12.7-mm (0.5-in) UBT guns, two 7.62-mm (0.3-in) ShKRS beam guns; 2,205 lb (1000 kg) bombs, increased to 6,614 lb (3000 kg)

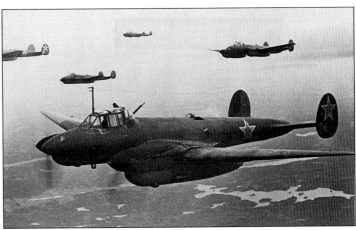

High-level bombing was never a forte of the Soviet air forces and in the bombing role the Pe-2 was confined largely to medium level and dive-bombing. The type proved to be an elusive target for German fighters when used in the ground support and attack roles. Total production reached 11,400 before ending in 1945.

Potez 63

It had always been assumed that the Potez 63.11 reconnaissance aircraft would operate under fighter protection. This seldom proved possible during the Battle of France when more than one in three of 700 were shot down in two months.

The brief operational history of the **Potez 63** series is dramatic for the courage of its crews and the magnitude of its part in the Battle of France in 1940. The type also served in greater numbers than any other French aircraft. Conceived to a 1934 requirement for a combined fighter director/day attack and night-fighter, the prototype **Potez 630-01** first flew on 25 April 1936 and displayed all the shortcomings of design compromise. Disorganisation, reorganisation and amalgamation in the French aircraft industry delayed production, but by the war 379 examples of five versions were in service, albeit approaching obsolescence: these were the **Potez 630** and **Potez 631** two/three-crew day and night-fighters, **Potez 633** two-seat light bombers, **Potez 637** three-crew reconnaissance aircraft and **Potez 63.11** three-crew army co-operation aircraft. Owing to their superficial resemblance to the German Bf 110 there were occasions when they were attacked by RAF and French fighters. Deliveries continued at an increasing rate after the beginning of the war, and by 10 May 1940 the type equipped fighter, bomber, reconnaissance and army co-operation units of the Armée de l'Air, as well as fighter squadrons of the Aéronavale. In the face of superior German fighter opposition they were called on to perform all manner of operations, suffering appalling loss. By the armistice only 663 (251 of them in North Africa) survived from a total of 1,115 delivered, roughly 400 lost in combat.

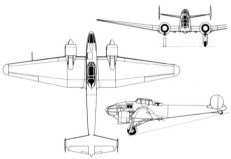

Potez 63.11

The Potez 63 was originally intended in three major versions: two-seat interceptor or escort fighter, two-seat night-fighter, and three-seat fighter equipped with radio to direct other fighters. Total production of the Potez 63 series was 1,395, including a number of undelivered Potez 63.11s seized and flown by the Luftwaffe.

Specification: Potez 631
Type: two/three-crew day and night-fighter
Powerplant: two 700-hp (522-kW) Gnome-Rhône 14 M4/MS radial pistons
Performance: max speed 275 mph (442 km/h) at 14,765 ft (4500 m); climb to 13,125 ft (4000 m) in 5.9 minutes; range 758 miles (1220 km)
Weights: empty 5,401 Lb (2450 kg); normal loaded 8,289 Lb (3760 kg)
Dimensions: span 52 ft 6 in (16.00 m); length 36 ft 4 in (11.07 m); height 11 ft 10½ in (3.62 m); wing area 351.98 sq ft (32.70 m²)
Armament: two fixed forward-firing 20-mm HS404 cannon and one flexible 7.5-mm (0.295-in) MAC 1934 machine-gun in rear cockpit, plus (optionally) four 7.5-mm (0.295-in) MAC 1934 guns in underwing packs

PZL P-11

Bearing the marking of No. 113 (Owls) Sqn, this P-11C was also one of the 1st Air Regiment's aircraft during the Polish campaign of September 1939. After a week's fighting, all unit insignia were painted over.

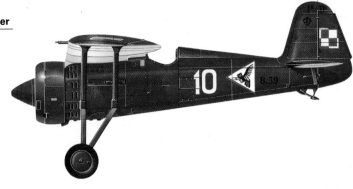

Initiated by the talented designer Ing. Zygmunt Pulawski, the Polish P series of monoplane fighters was characterised by a high gull-wing layout at a time when the rest of the world was still engrossed with wringing the last drop of performance out of the biplane formula. The series entered service with the Polish air force in the form of the initial P-7a during the winter of 1932-33. Production of the P-7 series amounted to 153 aircraft powered by the 485-hp (362-kW) Skoda-built Bristol Jupiter VIIF radial and typical performance included a speed of about 170 mph (274 km/h) at sea level. By the time the P-7 was in service, Pulawski had moved on to more refined things, and the prototype **P-11/I** first flew in September 1931. The first production version was the **P-11b** and this, powered by the 525-hp (392-kW) IAR-built Gnome-Rhône 9K radial, entered service in 1935. Developments then produced the **P-11F** with Gnome-Rhône 9Krse radial, and the **P-11a** and **P-11c** with the Skoda-built Bristol Mercury VI or Mercury VIS.2 radials. When Germany invaded Poland in September 1939, the Polish fighter arm had 128 P-11 aircraft deployed in six regiments.

The P-11 pilots fought with great gallantry, but their aircraft were totally outmoded by the Bf 109 and losses amounted to 46 PZL fighters in the first three days of the campaign. Production of all P-11s was 330 aircraft, and about 300 of the improved P-24 series had been produced for export.

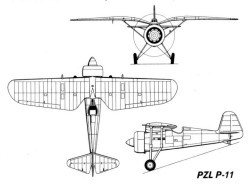

PZL P-11

Specification: PZL P-11c

Type: single-seat interceptor fighter
Powerplant: one 645-hp (481-kW) Skoda-built Bristol Mercury VIS.2 radial piston
Performance: max speed 242 mph (390 km/h) at 18,050 ft (5500 m); climb to 16,405 ft (5000 m) in 6.0 minutes; service ceiling 26,250 ft (8000 m); range 435 miles (700 km)
Weights: empty 2,529 Lb (1147 kg); max take-off 3,968 Lb (1800 kg)
Dimensions: span 35 ft 2 in (10.72 m); length 24 ft 9¼ in (7.55 m); height 9 ft 4½ in (2.85 m)
Armament: two forward-firing 7.7-mm (0.303-in) KM Wz33 machine-gun

Seen during 1957's National Aviation Days, this PZL P-11C belonged No. 121 (Winged Arrows) Squadron. The parasol fighter, although flown bravely by its Polish pilots, was no match for the Luftwaffe's Messerschmitts.

103

PZL P-23 Karas

This P-23 is from No. 42 (Bomber) Sqn, Army Pomorze. Restricted by their subordination to local army command, these bomber squadrons lost much of their value while awaiting suitable targets when they could have reinforced other hard-pressed forces.

Probably not significantly inferior to the Fairey Battle fielded by the RAF and Belgian air force, the **PZL P-23 Karas** (Crucian Carp) was a single-engined light bomber designed to meet the tactical requirements of the Polish army. The basic design was more than adequate, but the type's operational capabilities foundered on lack of power once the Bristol Pegasus had been specified. First flown in August 1934 as the **P-23/I** prototype with the 590-hp (440-kW) Pegasus IIM.2, the Karas entered service in June 1936 as the **P-23a** with the same engine. So low was performance with payload, however, that all 40 aircraft were soon converted into dual-control trainers. The first true operational variant was thus the **P-23b**, which had been involved by way of the **P-23/III** third prototype re-engined with the 680-hp (507-kW) Pegasus VIII. The P-23b was the major production model, 210 being built. The type entered service in 1937, and in September 1939 150 were operational in 12 squadrons of the Polish air force: five in the Bomber Brigade, and the other seven as reconnaissance units attached to the army staffs involved in trying to stem the rapid German advance. In 16

days about 112 P-23b bombers were lost, all but 22 in aerial combat. Much better capability was offered by the **P-43** developed version, which was powered by the 970-hp (724-kW) Gnome-Rhône 14 NO 1. All 54 P-43 aircraft were ordered by Bulgaria, although nine were retained briefly by Poland.

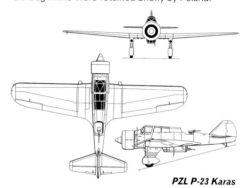

PZL P-23 Karas

A total of 118 PZL P-23 Karas reconnaissance bombers was available to the Polish air force on 1 September 1939. This aircraft flew with No. 22 (Bomber) Sqn of the Bomber Brigade, a unit which participated in the series of effective raids against the German 10th Army Group's armoured divisions between 4 and 8 September.

Specification: PZL P-23b Karas
Type: three-crew light bomber
Powerplant: one 680-hp (507-kW) PZL-built Bristol Pegasus VIII radial piston
Performance: max speed 186 mph (300 km/h) at 6,560 ft (2000 m); climb to 6,560 ft (2000 m) in 4.75 minutes; service ceiling 23,950 ft (7300 m); range 782 miles (1260 km)
Weights: empty 4,250 lb (1928 kg); normal loaded 7,716 lb (3400 kg)
Dimensions: span 45 ft 9¼ in (13.95 m); length 31 ft 9⅛ in (9.68 m); height 10 ft 10 in (3.30 m); wing area 288.5 sq ft (26.80 m²)
Armament: one forward-firing 7.7-mm (0.303-in) KM Wz33 machine-gun and single 7.7-mm (0.303-in) Vickers machine-guns in dorsal position and ventral gondola; 1,543 lb (700 kg) bombs

Reggiane Re.2000

Almost all the 170 Re.2000s produced went to foreign air forces, namely those of Sweden and Hungary. One of those flown by the Regia Aeronautica was this Re.2000 GA Series IIIa of the 377ª Squadriglia Autonomo based at Palermo in March 1942.

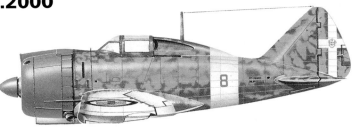

Desperately handicapped by the lack of an indigenous inline engine suitable for fighter aircraft, Italian aircraft designers before the war were obliged to persevere with second-rate radial engines, and the **Re.2000** was ample example of this handicap, representing only a marginal improvement over the Macchi C.200. The prototype Re.2000 was flown on 24 May 1939. As production got under way the Italian government cancelled its order, with the result that Reggiane decided to complete the first 188 aircraft at private expense so as to offer for export an off-the-shelf fighter (astonishingly, in January 1940 the UK negotiated an order for a batch, 'approved' by Germany). In the event, 70 aircraft were purchased by Hungary, these aircraft being designated **Re.2000 Series I**. As soon as Italy entered the war the government order was reinstated, none being delivered to the UK. As the only aircraft readily adaptable to accommodate extra fuel, the Re.2000 was selected to fly directly from Italy to East Africa to cover the Italian colonies. First deliveries to the Regia Aeronautica were to the 3º Stormo in Sicily in 1941, the Series I aircraft being mainly confined

to home defence. Only 10 **Series III** aircraft, converted for catapult launching from Italian warships, were delivered. The Re.2000 served longer in Hungary, with the 1/1 and 2/4 Squadrons of the Hungarian 2nd Air Brigade at Szolnok and Kolozsvar on the Russian Front. A total of 60 Re.2000s was supplied to Sweden and known as the **J 20**.

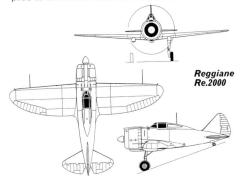

Reggiane Re.2000

Specification:
Reggiane Re.2000 Series I
Type: single-seat fighter
Powerplant: one 985-hp (735-kW) Piaggio PXI RC 40 radial piston
Performance: max speed 329 mph (530 km/h) at 16,405 ft (5000 m); climb to 13,125 ft (4000 m) in 45 minutes; service ceiling 30,510 ft (9300 m); range 708 miles (1140 km)
Weights: empty 4,563 Lb (2070 kg); max take-off 6,349 Lb (2880 kg)
Dimensions: span 36 ft 1 in (11.00 m); length 26 ft 2½ in (8.00 m); height 10 ft 6 in (3.20 m); wing area 219.6 sq ft (20.40 m²)
Armament: two synchronised 12.7-mm (0.5-in) Breda SAFAT machine-gun in nose

Production during 1939-40 of the highly manoeuvrable Re.2000 – unashamedly copied from the Sikorsky P-35 – totalled 380, plus two prototypes. This included the 192 built under licence-production in Hungary by MAVAG under the name Heja.

Republic P-47 Thunderbolt

P-47s were used by many Allied air forces in World War II, notably the British, French and Russian. This American P-47D-30 is from the 512th Fighter Squadron, 406th Fighter Group, seen at Nordholz in the summer of 1945.

Evolved from the radial-powered P-35, the big **Republic P-47** became one of America's three outstanding fighters of the war, perpetuating a preference in 1939-40 for air-cooled radial engines. First flown on 6 May 1941, the **XP-47B** was designed around the 2,000-hp (1492-kW) Pratt & Whitney R-2800 with exhaust-driven turbocharger in the rear fuselage; armament was eight 0.5-in (12.7-mm) machine-guns in the wings. Some 171 production **P-47B**s were built with minor improvements and a top speed of 429 mph (691 km/h), this version being brought to the UK in January 1943 by the 56th and 78th Fighter Groups; they were first flown in combat on 8 April, flying escort for B-17s. Early P-47s had poor climb and manoeuvrability, but were popular due to their ability to survive heavy battle damage. A lengthened fuselage and provision for an underfuselage drop tank identified the **P-47C**. The major version (12,602 built) was the **P-47D** with water injection power boost and cutdown rear fuselage with 'bubble' hood on late subvariants. P-47Ds served in the UK, Mediterranean and Far East; in Burma, 16 RAF squadrons flew the P-47B (**Thunderbolt Mk I**) and P-47D (**Mk II**), with

826 delivered. The **P-47M** with improved turbocharger and a top speed of 473 mph (762 km/h) reached Europe at the end of 1944. The **P-47N** with blunt-tipped, enlarged wing and increased fuel capacity was developed for service in the Pacific; 1,816 were produced, escorting B-29s in their raids.

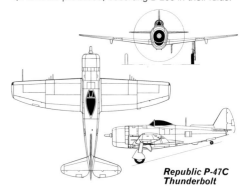

Republic P-47C Thunderbolt

This P-47 served with the US Eighth Air Force and was based in England. The white paint on the engine cowling and tail was applied to prevent confusion with the German Fw 190, which was similar in appearance. Some 15,675 P-47s were produced.

Specification:
Republic P-47D-25 (Thunderbolt Mk II)
Type: single-seat long-range fighter
Powerplant: one 2,300-hp (1716-kW) Pratt & Whitney R-2800-59 radial piston
Performance: max speed 428 mph (689 km/h) at 30,000 ft (9145 m); climb to 20,000 ft (6095 m) in 9.0 minutes; service ceiling 42,000 ft (12800 m); range 1,260 miles (2028 km)
Weights: empty 10,000 Lb (4536 kg); max take-off 19,400 Lb (8800 kg)
Dimensions: span 40 ft 9½ in (12.43 m); length 36 ft 1¾ in (11.01 m); height 14 ft 2 in (4.32 m); wing area 300.0 sq ft (27.87 m²)
Armament: eight 0.5-in (12.7-mm) machine-guns in wings; two 1,000-lb (454-kg) bombs

Savoia-Marchetti SM.79 Sparviero

The 'Electric Man' device on this Sparviero identifies it as an aircraft of the 193ª Squadriglia BT, 87° Gruppo BT, 30° Stormo BT, based in Sicily during 1940 and 1941.

The three-engined **SM.79 Sparviero** (Sparrow) was developed from the SM.81 in 1934 as a commercial entry for the MacRobertson England-Australia race. It was not finished in time to compete and made its maiden flight in October, with the second prototype completed as a bomber. Some Sparvieri served in Spain, and **SM.79-I**s joined the Regia Aeronautica in 1937 as a medium bomber and later as a torpedo-bomber. By 1939 a total of 11 *stormi* were equipped with the SM.79-I powered by Alfa Romeo radials. A total of 389 aircraft was deployed in Italy, Albania and the Aegean; by June 1940 the number had increased to 14 *stormi* with 594 aircraft. Of these, three *stormi* were located in Italy, two in Sardinia, four in Libya and five in Sicily. They participated in the short-lived campaign against France and in the Balkans, as well as supporting Italian operations in the Western Desert. Contrary to propaganda, the Sparviero was not easy meat for British fighters in 1940-41 and, had it not been for a light bomb load, their presence in large numbers would have presented problems for the British in North Africa, particularly with the arrival of the **SM.79bis** with 1,000-hp (746-kW)

Piaggio P.XI radials. Attrition in North Africa reduced the number of SM.79s available, and at the time of the Torch landings only 112 were available. Some 1,330 Sparvieri were produced, including cleaned-up **SM.79ters** (**SM.79-III**) from 1944.

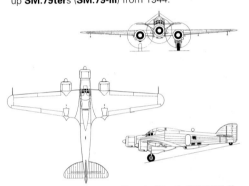

Savoia-Marchetti SM.79-II

Specification: Savoia-Marchetti SM.79-I Sparviero
Type: four/five-crew bomber
Powerplant: three 780-hp (582-kW) Alfa Romeo 126 RC 34 radial pistons
Performance: max speed 267 mph (430 km/h) at 13,125 ft (4000 m); climb to 13,125 ft (4000 m) in 13.25 minutes; ceiling 21,325 ft (6500 m); range 2,051 miles (3300 km)
Weights: empty 15,322 Lb (6950 kg); max take-off 23,644 Lb (10725 kg)
Dimensions: span 69 ft 6⅔ in (21.20 m); length 53 ft 1¾ in (16.20 m); height 13 ft 5⅛ in (4.10 m); wing area 664.2 sq ft (61.70 m²)
Armament: 12.7-mm (0.5-in) Breda SAFAT machine-gun in forward, dorsal and ventral positions plus two 7.7-mm (0.303-in) Lewis gun; max five 551-lb (250-kg) bombs

The Italians achieved outstanding success with the torpedo-carrying Sparviero. Numerous British ships were sunk in a series of brilliant attacks, including the battleship HMS Malaya and carrier HMS Argus which were struck by aircraft of the celebrated 132° Gruppo.

Savoia-Marchetti SM.81

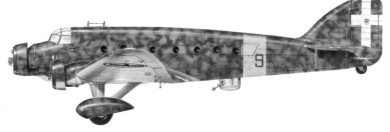

This Savoia-Marchetti SM.81 served with the 245ª Squadriglia Hasporto, Krivoy Rog, Ukraine, in September 1941. It was part of the Corpo de Spedizione Italiano in Russia, an Italian contribution to Germany's invasion of Russia.

Similar in concept to the German Ju 52/3m, Italy's **SM.81** was developed from the SM.73 transport as a medium bomber and first appeared in 1934. It entered production with three 670-hp (500-kW) Piaggio P.X radials, joining the 7º, 9º, 13º and 15º Stormi in 1935. Many of these aircraft served in the Ethiopian campaign as bombers and transports, and from 1936 in the Spanish Civil War. By 1939, the SM.81 was widely regarded as obsolescent upon the arrival of the excellent SM.79, yet when Italy entered the conflict in 1940 the Regia Aeronautica still fielded 304 serviceable SM.81s, of which 147 were based in the Mediterranean and 59 in East Africa as bombers, and the remainder as transports. Some updating of the aircraft was attempted with the installation of Alfa Romeo 125 RC 35 and 126 RC 34, and Gnome-Rhône K14 radials, but in service the aircraft remained fundamentally unchanged. In East Africa SM.81s of the 4º and 29º Gruppi were active in raids over Khartoum, Port Sudan and Aden, and in support of the Italian invasion of Somaliland, but eventually suffered losses to extinction. In the Mediterranean, Aegean-based SM.81s of the 39º Stormo made a number

of attacks on the British fleet, but in the main SM.81 operations in the Western Desert were confined to transport duties. During the war the SM.81 equipped a total of 24 *squadriglie* of the 7º, 8º, 9º, 14º, 15º, 37º, 38º and 39º Stormi as bombers, and of the 18º Stormo as transports.

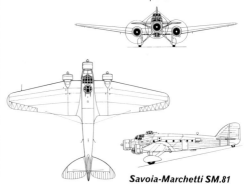

Savoia-Marchetti SM.81

Similar in design concept to the German Ju 52/3m, the big SM.81 retained its bombing capability longer, and was employed in that capacity well into the war, particularly in Italian East Africa. By the time of the Italian armistice in September 1943, the aircraft had almost disappeared from service.

Specification: Savoia-Marchetti SM.81 Series 5
Type: five-crew medium bomber
Powerplant: three 780-hp (582-kW) Alfa Romeo 126 RC 34 radial pistons
Performance: max speed 209 mph (336 km/h) at 16,405 ft (5000 m); climb to 16,405 ft (5000 m) in 19.27 minutes; ceiling 21,600 ft (6600 m); range 1,243 miles (2000 km)
Weights: empty 14,991 Lb (6800 kg); max take-off 23,148 lb (10500 kg)
Dimensions: span 78 ft 8¾ in (24.00 m); length 64 ft 3 in (19.58 m); height 14 ft 4 in (4.37 m); wing area 1,001.1 sq ft (93.00 m²)
Armament: two 7.7-mm (0.303-in) Breda SAFAT machine-guns in each of dorsal and ventral turrets, and one in each of two beam positions; four 1,102-lb (500-kg) bombs

Short Stirling

Shown here is a Stirling Mk I of No. 149 (East India) Sqn based at Mildenhall in January 1942. This squadron flew its Stirlings in the first of the famous 1,000-bomber raids on Germany.

The **Short Stirling** was the first of Bomber Command's trio of four-engined heavy bombers that mounted the great night offensive over Europe during the last four years of the war. Designed to a 1936 specification, the Stirling was flown as a half-scale prototype in 1938, followed by the full-scale prototype which was destroyed on its initial flight in May 1939. Production deliveries were first made to No. 7 Squadron in August 1940 (at the height of the Battle of Britain) and the Stirling flew its maiden operation on 10-11 February 1941. The type first bombed Berlin two months later. The **Stirling Mk I**, (756 produced) was powered by Hercules XI radials, and the **Mk II** with Wright Cyclones did not progress beyond the prototype stage. The **Mk III** was powered by Hercules XVIs and, with 875 built (plus many Mk Is converted), constituted the main bomber variant, and introduced the two-gun dorsal turret. Stirlings were the first operational aircraft to carry the original form of Oboe radar in 1941, and in August 1942 took part in the first Pathfinder operations. Two posthumous VCs were won by Stirling pilots (Flight Sergeant R. H. Middleton of No. 149 Squadron and Flight Sergeant A. L. Aaron

of No. 218 Squadron), both during raids on northern Italy. The **Mk IV** (577 built) was a transport/glider tug without nose and dorsal turrets, and was used on operations by the airborne forces during 1945. The **Mk V** transport (160 built), without armament, joined the RAF in January 1945.

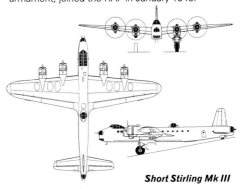

Short Stirling Mk III

Specification: Short Stirling Mk III
Type: seven/eight-crew night heavy bomber
Powerplant: four 1,650-hp (1231-kW) Bristol Hercules XVI radial pistons
Performance: max speed 270 mph (435 km/h) at 14,500 ft (4420 m); service ceiling 17,000 ft (5180 m); range with 14,000-lb (6350-kg) bomb load 590 miles (949 km)
Weights: empty 43,200 Lb (19596 kg); max take-off 70,000 Lb (31790 kg)
Dimensions: span 99 ft 1 in (30.20 m0; length 87 ft 3 in (26.50 m); height 22 ft 9 in (6.93 m); wing area 1,460.0 sq ft (135.60 m²)
Armament: two 0.303-in (7.7-mm) machine-guns in each nose and dorsal turrets, and four 0.303-in (7.7-mm) guns in tail turret; 14,000 lb (6350 kg) bombs

The Stirling always gave the impression of great size, on account of its huge undercarriage. Capable of carrying up to 14,000 lb (6350 kg) of bombs, its performance was, however, disappointing, and the aircraft was never as popular in service as the Halifax and Lancaster. Stirling bombers equipped 15 squadrons.

Short Sunderland

Festooned with ASV (air to surface vessel) radar aerials, Sunderlands ranged far and wide over the Atlantic and Indian Oceans throughout the war in their endless search for enemy submarines and surface raiders.

The big, graceful **Short Sunderland**, which played such a vital part in the Battle of the Atlantic, was a military development of the famous pre-war 'C'-class Empire flying-boat. It made its maiden flight in October 1937 and joined Nos 210 and 230 Squadrons during the following summer. Production continued until October 1945, by which time 721 aircraft had been produced. The **Sunderland Mk I** featured a prominent forward step in the planing bottom; **Mk IIs**, which first flew in 1941, introduced a two-gun dorsal turret, and the **Mk III** of 1942 incorporated a shallower forward step in the planing bottom. All these versions were powered by four 1,065-hp (795-kW) Bristol Pegasus XVIII radials, and the first powerplant change came with the **Mk V** of 1943 with Pratt & Whitney Twin Wasps. The **Mk IV** (later known as the **Seaford**) did not enter service during the war. Affectionately known as the 'Flying Porcupine', on account of its heavy defensive armament, the Sunderland flew with 17 squadrons of the RAF based in the UK, the Middle East, the Far East, Iceland, Gibraltar and West Africa. The type flew countless hours protecting convoys in the Atlantic, rescued survivors from torpedoed ships, hunted and sank a number of U-boats (the first on 30 January 1940), and assisted in a number of transport operations, notably during the evacuations of Norway, Greece and Crete.

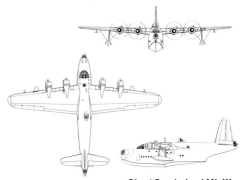

Short Sunderland Mk III

Its pre-war commercial ancestry made the Sunderland a graceful sight, evidenced by this Mk III. Sunderland crews maintained a long and lonely vigil over vast areas of ocean throughout the war; bristling with machine-guns, they frequently gave a good account of themselves when attacked.

Specification: Short Sunderland Mk V
Type: 13-crew maritime reconnaissance flying-boat
Powerplant: four 1,200-hp (895-kW) Pratt & Whitney Twin Wasp R-1830 radial pistons
Performance: max speed 213 mph (343 km/h) at 5,000 ft (1525 m); initial climb rate 840 ft (256 m) per minute; ceiling 17,900 ft (5455 m); range 2,980 miles (4795 km)
Weights: empty 37,000 lb (16783 kg); max take-off 65,000 lb (29482 kg)
Dimensions: span 112 ft 9½ in (34.36 m); length 85 ft 4 in (26.01 m); height 32 ft 10½ in (10.01 m); wing area 1,487.0 sq ft (138.14 m²)
Armament: four 0.303-in (7.7-mm) machine-guns in nose, four in tail turret, two in bow turret, two 0.5-in (12.7-mm) guns in beam; 2,000 Lb (907 kg) bombs

Sukhoi Su-2

By 1942 the Su-2 was receiving a battering from German fighters and flak due to its poor performance and manoeuvrability. The aircraft shown here belonged to a second-line unit in the Sverdlovsk area in 1942-43.

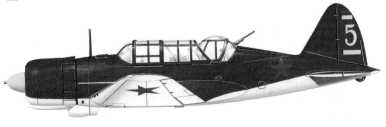

Pavel **Sukhoi**'s **Su-2** proved something of a disappointment, as did many of the world's single-engined attack aircraft of the late 1930s, being in the main undergunned, underpowered and overweight. In much the same class as the ill-fated Fairey Battle, the prototype **ANT-51** (so-called after A. N. Tupolev, in whose bureau Sukhoi worked) had flown in August 1937 with an M-62 radial, a Russian copy of the Wright Cyclone. Later aircraft were powered by M-87s, developed from the French Gnome-Rhône 14K, before the aircraft entered production in 1940 as the **BB-1** medium-range attack bomber. Maximum speed with bomb load was around 230 mph (370 km/h) and when the type was faced by German fighters in 1941 this proved disastrously inadequate, so a new version with 1,000-hp (746-kW) Shvetsov M-88B radial was quickly introduced as the **Su-2** (reflecting the new Russian practice of recognising the designer). Without the heavy armour protection of the Il-2 and with scarcely any worthwhile gun defence, the Su-2 continued to provide easy meat for Luftwaffe and flak alike. Although an Su-2 was flown with a 2,100-hp (1567-kW) M-90, which increased the speed to around 340 mph (547 km/h) with load, the decision was taken to abandon the Su-2 in favour of the rugged Il-2, for which enormous manufacturing facilities had been prepared.

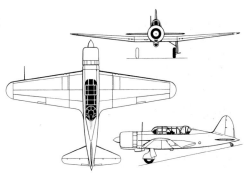

Sukhoi Su-2

Specification: Sukhoi Su-2
Type: two-seat attack bomber
Powerplant: one 1,000-hp (746-hp) Shvetsov M-88B radial piston
Performance: max speed 283 mph (455 km/h) at 8,200 ft (2500 m); service ceiling 28,870 ft (8800 m); range 739 miles (1190 km)
Weights: empty 6,614 lb (3000 kg); max take-off 9,645 lb (4375 kg)
Dimensions: span 46 ft 11 in (14.30 m); length 33 ft 7½ in (10.25 m); wing area 312.1 sq ft (29.00 m²)
Armament: four 7.62-mm (0.3-in) ShKAS machine-guns in wings and one or two 7.62-mm (0.3-in) ShKAS machine-guns in dorsal turret; 882 Lb (400 kg) bombs internal and 1,323 Lb (600 kg) external

Although highly regarded by the air regiments to which it was assigned, the German invasion of June 1941 revealed that such light bombers, operating at low and medium altitudes, were vulnerable unless provided with powerful fighter cover. The last Su-2s are thought to have been delivered in 1943.

Supermarine Spitfire

The Spitfire was widely used by the USAAF, with over 20,351 produced. Most were Mk Vs and Mk IXs, but this aircraft, shown in desert finish, was a Mk VIII flown by the CO of the 308th Fighter Squadron, 31st FG, in Italy, 1944.

First flown on 5 March 1936, the **Spitfire Mk I** with Merlin II engine entered RAF service in August 1938, and was heavily committed in the Battle of Britain. The **Mk II** with Merlin XII followed in September 1940, and the **Mk IIB** was armed with two 20-mm guns and four machine-guns. The photo-reconnaissance **Mk IV** was followed in March 1941 by the **Mk V** (6,479 produced) with 1,440-hp (1074-kW) Merlin 45; the **Mk VC** fighter-bomber could carry one 500-lb (227-kg) or two 250-Lb (113-kg) bombs. The **Mk VB** was the mainstay of Fighter Command between mid-1941 and mid-1942 when the **Mk IX**, with 1,660-hp (1238-kW) Merlin 61 with two-stage, two-speed supercharger joined the RAF. The **Mk VI** and **Mk VII** were high-altitude fighters with extended wingtips, and the fully tropicalised **Mk VIII** fighter and fighter-bomber was used principally in the Mediterranean and Far East. The **Mk X** and **Mk XI** were unarmed photo-reconnaissance versions and the **Mk XVI**, with a top speed of 405 mph (652 km/h), was produced in fighter and fighter-bomber versions. All the foregoing (18,298 were built) were powered by the Rolls-Royce Merlin. The first with 1,735-hp (1294-kW)

Griffon IV was the **Mk XII**, introduced in 1943 to counter the Fw 190. It was followed by the 2,050-hp (1529-kW) Griffon 65-powered **Mk XIV** fighter and fighter-bomber. The late-war fighter-reconnaissance **Mk XVIII** had a top speed of 442 mph (712 km/h). In the Fleet Air Arm, **Seafires** served in large numbers with both Merlin and Griffon engines.

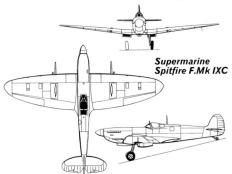

Supermarine Spitfire F.Mk IXC

The immortal Spitfire is seen here in its Mk VB form and in the markings of No. 222 Squadron. The sleek original aircraft had been tailored around the then-new Rolls-Royce Merlin engine, and the distinctive elliptical wings housed eight machine-guns, all firing outside of the propeller disc.

Specification:
Supermarine Spitfire Mk VB
Type: single-seat interceptor fighter
Powerplant: one 1,440-hp (1074-kW) Rolls-Royce Merlin 45/46/50 inline piston
Performance: max speed 374 mph (602 km/h) at 13,000 ft (3960 m); climb to 20,000 ft (6095 m) in 7.5 minutes; service ceiling 37,000 ft (11280 m); range on internal fuel 470 miles (756 km)
Weights: empty 5,100 lb (2313 kg); max take-off 6,785 lb (3078 kg)
Dimensions: span 36 ft 10 in (11.23 m); length 29 ft 11 in (9.11 m); height 11 ft 5 in (3.48 m); wing area 242.0 sq ft (22.48 m²)
Armament: two 20-mm cannon and four 0.303-in (7.7-mm) machine-guns in wings

Tupolev SB-2

This late production SB-2bis was powered by the M-103 inline engine. This version had a top speed of 280 mph (451 km/h), but was painfully undergunned and suffered enormous losses in the opening months of Germany's Operation Barbarossa.

In much the same category as the British Bristol Blenheim, the **Tupolev SB-2** was also a light twin-engined bomber with three-man crew. Designed by the bureau led by A. N. Tupolev, the prototype **ANT-40** (later designated **SB-1**, 'SB' indicating fast bomber) flew on 7 October 1934, and the type entered service early in 1936 as the SB-2 powered by two 750-hp (560-kW) VK-100 inline engines, which were in effect Russian copies of the Hispano-Suiza 12Y. Of all-metal stressed-skin construction, the SB-2 fought during the Spanish Civil War in 1936-39 when its 280-mph (450-km/h) top speed rendered it almost immune from interception by Nationalist fighters. It also served with the Chinese Central Government air force against Japan during 1938-39. In the Winter War of 1939-40 between the Soviet Union and Finland, the SB-2 was already obsolescent and suffered heavily, in general on account of the effects of the harsh weather conditions on the liquid-cooled engines. Nevertheless, a new version, the **SB-2bis** with 1,100-hp (821-kW) M-100A engines, began to be delivered in 1939 and, although production was phased out in 1942, this variant continued to serve

until the end of the war, being employed as a night-fighter in the last two years. The SB-2 was built in greater numbers than any comparable light twin-engined bomber of its time: production of all types was stated to be around 6,500, the bulk of these being produced during 1941-42.

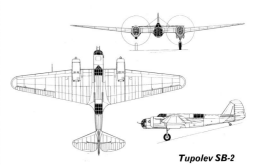

Tupolev SB-2

Often compared with the Bristol Blenheim, the SB-2 was in fact an older design, being the first Russian operational aircraft of metal stressed-skin construction. It was ineptly flown during the Russo-Finnish Winter War of 1939-40 and suffered heavy losses at the hands of determined Finnish pilots.

Tupolev Tu-2

The Tu-2 underwent relatively little design modification during its long service life, which reflected a sound concept but was also evidence of the Soviet need to achieve uninterrupted production of numbers of proven aircraft.

The **Tupolev Tu-2** must be regarded as one of the best Russian aircraft to be produced during the war, in much the same class as the American B-25 and B-26 bombers, although reflecting a number of features regarded as outmoded in the West. First flown as the **ANT-58** prototype in October 1940, the type incorporated many of the fruits of early wartime experience. Efforts to simplify the design for quantity production led to the **ANT-60**. The Tu-2 was still undergoing flight development when Germany invaded the Soviet Union in the summer of 1941, and the first service deliveries were not made until a year later. The heavily armed and armoured Tu-2, which was powered by the excellent 1,850-hp (1380-kW) Shvetsov ASh-82 FN radial giving a top speed of 342 mph (550 km/h) at medium level, remained largely unchanged throughout its production life (which lasted until 1948). It began to appear in large numbers at around the time of the murderous Stalingrad campaign. In the course of the great tank battles around Kursk during July 1943, the 23-mm cannon was introduced for attacks on the less-heavily armoured German vehicles, although it proved inadequate to deal with enemy tanks. Renowned for its rugged structure, the Tu-2 was extremely popular in service, the engines in particular being regarded as among the most reliable of any produced during the war. Difficulties at the factories resulted in only 1,100 Tu-2s and refined **Tu-2S**s being delivered before the end of the war.

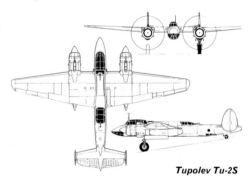

Tupolev Tu-2S

The Tu-2 was one of Russia's outstanding aircraft of the war, remaining in production from 1942 until 1948. This early Tu-2S features broad ailerons and augmented port fin. The type's bomb load in later aircraft was increased to 6,614 lb (3000 kg). Its nearest Western equivalent was probably the North American B-25.

Specification: Tupolev Tu-2
Type: four-crew attack bomber
Powerplant: two 1,850-hp (1380-kW) Shvetsov ASh-82FN radial pistons
Performance: max speed 342 mph (550 km/h) at 10,825 ft (3300 m); initial climb rate 2,295 ft (700 m) per minute; service ceiling 31,170 ft (9500 m); range 1,553 miles (2500 km)
Weights: empty 18,254 lb (8280 kg); max take-off 28,219 lb (12800 kg)
Dimensions: span 61 ft 10½ in (18.86 m); length 45 ft 3¾ in (13.80 m); height 13 ft 9½ in (4.20 m); wing area 525.3 sq ft (48.8 m²)
Armament: single 12.7-mm (0.5-in) UBT machine-guns in forward dorsal, rear dorsal & ventral positions, two 20-mm ShVAK cannon in wings; 5,004 Lb (2270 kg) bombs

Vickers Wellington

Typical of the Wellington night bomber versions was this Mk IC of No. 150 Sqn, based at Newton in December 1940. This squadron flew the bomber from October 1940 until October 1944, taking them to North Africa in late 1942.

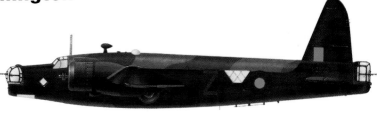

Employing the efficient geodetic lattice structure, the twin-engined **Vickers Wellington** served with Bomber Command until 1943. Designed to meet a 1932 requirement, the type first flew on 15 June 1936, and in its **Mk I** form with Pegasus radials joined the RAF (No. 9 Squadron) in October 1938. The **Mk IC** with Nash and Thompson nose and tail gun turrets followed, together with the Merlin-powered **Mk II** and Hercules III- or XI-powered **Mk III**, and by 1939 six squadrons were flying the Wellington. Early daylight raids resulted in heavy losses owing to the type's large defenceless arcs, and in 1940 the aircraft joined the night bombing force. On 1 April 1941 a Wellington dropped the RAF's first 4,000-lb (1814-kg) bomb. Subsequent bomber versions included the Twin Wasp-powered **Mk IV**, and **Mks V** and **VI** high-altitude aircraft with pressure cabins; the latter versions did not see combat service. The **Mk X** with Hercules XVIIIs was the final bomber version, and the last raid by Bomber Command Wellingtons took place on 8-9 October 1943. Wellingtons had been flying on maritime duties, the **DW.Mk I** with large mine-exploding hoops having operated in 1940 and **Mk IC** minelayers soon after. Coastal Command versions included the **GR.Mk VIII** with Pegasus engines and ASV radar, and the **GR.Mks XI** and **XII** with Hercules, Leigh Light and two torpedoes. The **T.Mks XVII** and **XVIII** were trainers, and many Mk Xs were converted to 'flying classrooms'. The **C.Mks XV** and **XVI** were transport conversions of the Mk IC.

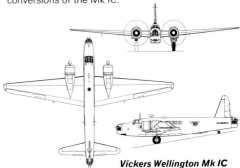

Vickers Wellington Mk IC

Dr Barnes Wallis' prolific drawing board produced the famous Wellington bomber, which served throughout the war in a variety of roles. It was the best of the RAF's night bombers in the early months of the war and served on a total of 57 squadrons in various versions. Some 11,461 aircraft were produced.

Vought F4U Corsair

This F4U-1A (without carrier equipment) served with No. 18 Sqn of the Royal New Zealand Air Force, flying from Bougainville in the Solomons in 1945, when the Corsair was this air force's principal fighter.

Distinctive yet not unattractive with its inverted gull wing, the **Vought F4U Corsair** was unquestionably the best shipborne fighter of the war, and gained an 11:1 kill:loss ratio in the Pacific. Designed by Tex B. Beisel, the **XF4U-1** was flown on 29 May 1940, the first production **F4U-1**s being delivered to VF-12 in October 1942, although most of the early aircraft went to the US Marine Corps. It was a land-based US Marine squadron, VMF-124, that first flew the Corsair into action, on 13 February 1943 over Bougainville. Additional production lines were set up by Brewster and Goodyear, these companies producing the **F3A-1** and **FG-1**, respectively. To improve the pilot's field of vision, later aircraft introduced a raised cockpit, and the **F4U-1C** had four 20-mm cannon. The **F4U-1D**, **FG-1D** and **F3A-1D** were powered by water-injection boosted R-2800-8W engines, and could carry two 1,000-lb (454-kg) bombs or eight 5-in (127-mm) rockets under the wings. Late in the war a night-fighter version, the **XF4U-2**, saw limited service with VFN-75 and VFN-101. Wartime production of the Corsair (which continued until 1952 with later versions) reached 4,120 F4U-1s, 735 F3A-1s and 3,808 FG-1s; of these, 2,012 were supplied to the UK's Fleet Air Arm and 370 to New Zealand. It was the Royal Navy's **Corsair Mk II**s of No. 1834 Squadron that were the first Corsairs to operate from a carrier when, on 3 April 1944, they took part in operations against the *Tirpitz*.

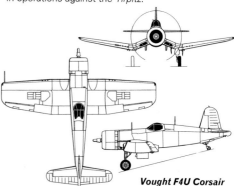

Vought F4U Corsair

Regarded as the best shipboard fighter of the war, the F-4U is seen here carrying a 1,000-lb (454-kg) bomb under the fuselage. The unusual wing configuration allowed retractable landing gear to be used with the engine's large-diameter propeller, the gear being located at the 'pinion' point of the wing.

Specification: Vought F4U-1 Corsair
Type: single-seat shipboard fighter
Powerplant: one 2,000-hp (1492-kW) Pratt & Whitney R-2800-8 radial piston
Performance: max speed 417 mph (671 km/h) at 19,900 ft (6066 m); initial climb rate 2,890 ft (881 m) per minute; service ceiling 36,900 ft (11245 m); range 1,015 miles (1633 km)
Weights: empty 8,982 Lb (4074 kg); max take-off 14,000 Lb (6350 kg)
Dimensions: span 41 ft 0 in (12.50 m); length 33 ft 4½ in (10.17 m); height 16 ft 1 in (4.90 m); wing area 314.0 sq ft (29.17 m²)
Armament: six forward-firing 0.5-in (12.7-mm) machine-guns in wings

Westland Lysander

No. 13 Sqn, one of whose Lysander Mk IIs is depicted here, supported the British Expeditionary Force in France at the outbreak of war. The squadron suffered heavily during the German attack in the west of May 1940.

First flown in prototype form during June 1936, the **Westland Lysander** was a two-seat high-wing monoplane army co-operation aircraft with excellent STOL capabilities. The first production series was the **Lysander Mk I**, and aircraft of this version entered service in late 1938 with No. 16 Squadron, based at Old Sarum. Lysanders went on to equip some 30 RAF squadrons, and these served in Europe, the Middle East and the Far East. The type was built in three marks distinguished mainly by the different powerplants used. The Lysander Mk I featured the 890-hp (664-kW) Bristol Mercury XII radial; the Lysander **Mk II**, which was built in the UK by Westland and in Canada by the National Steel Car Corporation, had the 950-hp (709-kW) Bristol Perseus XII radial; and the Lysander **Mk III**, which was also built in the UK and Canada, used the 870-hp (649-kW) Mercury XX or Mercury XXX radial. The Lysander operated in its intended role for only a short time in the war, European operations confirming that such large and relatively slow aircraft were deathtraps in the presence of determined opposition, both ground and air. However, the type went on to a notably successful second career in air-sea rescue, radar calibration and, perhaps most significantly, agent dropping and recovery in occupied Europe. Total production amounted to 1,368 aircraft.

Westland Lysander

Specification: Westland Lysander Mk I

Type: two-seat army co-op and short-range tactical recce
Powerplant: one 890-hp (664-kW) Bristol Mercury XII radial piston
Performance: max speed 229 mph (369 km/h) at 10,000 ft (3050 m); climb to 10,000 ft (3050 m) in 5.5 minutes; service ceiling 26,000 ft (7925 m); range 600 miles (966 km)
Weights: empty 4,065 lb (1844 kg); normal loaded 5,920 lb (2685 kg)
Dimensions: span 50 ft 0 in (15.24 m); length 30 ft 6 in (9.30 m); height 11 ft 6 in (3.51 m); wing area 260.0 sq ft (24.15 m²)
Armament: two forward-firing 0.303-in (7.7-mm) machine-guns in wheel fairings and the rear cockpit; eight 20-lb (907-kg) bombs on stub winglet

Possessing an excellent short-field performance, the Lysander proved a useful army operation and short-range reconnaissance aircraft, and served on many wartime fronts. These aircraft, probably of No. 208 Sqn, are seen over the Suez Canal.

117

Yakovlev Yak-1/-3/-7/-9

Replaced by later Yak developments in 1944, the Yak-3 continued to serve, particularly as personal aircraft of senior officers. This example was flown by Major General G. N. Zakharov, commanding the 303rd Fighter Aviation Division.

It is said that 37,000 Yakovlev fighters were produced during the war, of which the vast majority were **Yak-9**s, superb aircraft that could outfight the German Bf 109G as early as the time of the Stalingrad campaign. Developed progressively from the **Yak-1** (which first flew in March 1939), through the Yak-7B which served from early 1942, the Yak-9 was first flown in its production form in the summer of that year, returning a speed of 373 mph (600 km/h). Numerous versions of this versatile fighter were developed, including the **Yak-9T** anti-tank fighter with 1,260-hp (940-kW) Klimov VK-105PF inline engine and 37-mm hub-firing cannon, the **Yak-9B** fighter-bomber with provision for 882 Lb (400 kg) of bombs, the **Yak-9D** long-range fighter and the **Yak-9DD** very-long-range escort fighter, the latter being flown as escort for USAAF bombers on shuttle raids between the UK and the Soviet Union late in the war. The **Yak-9U** fighter, with 1,650-hp (1231-kW) VK-107A engine and a top speed of 435 mph (700 km/h), was the final version to see combat during the war and represented the point at which Soviet technology may be said to have finally caught up with that of the West, and

came to be much respected by the best Luftwaffe pilots in their final generation of Bf 109K and Fw 190D fighters. When the type was phased out of production in mid-1943, a total of 8,721 series aircraft of all versions had been completed.

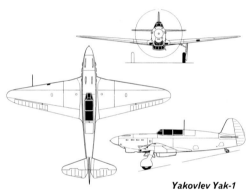

Yakovlev Yak-1

In this formation of Yak-9Ds of a Guards Regiment in the Crimea, the nearest aircraft is flown by Colonel M. V. Avdyeyev, holder of the Gold Star of a Hero of the Soviet Union. The two insignia on the Yak's nose are the Guards' unit insignia and the Order of the Red Banner.

Specification:
Yakovlev Yak-9U
Type: single-seat fighter
Powerplant: one 1,650-hp (1231-kW) VK-107A inline piston
Performance: max speed 435 mph (700 km/h) at 22,640 ft (6900 m); initial climb rate 4,920 ft (1500 m) per minute; service ceiling 35,925 ft (10950 m); range 609 miles (980 m)
Weights: empty 5,093 Lb (2310 kg); normal loaded 6,989 Lb (3170 kg)
Dimensions: span 32 ft 9¾ in (10.00 m); length 28 ft 6½ in (8.70 m); height 8 ft 0 in (2.44 m)
Armament: one 23-mm hub-firing VYa-23V cannon and two 12.7-mm (0.3-in) UBS machine-guns; two 220-lb (100-kg) bombs

Yokosuka D4Y 'Judy'

This Yokosuka D4Y3 Suisei Model 33 belonged to the 601st Kokutai. Later versions of the D4Y3 were frequently equipped with three solid-fuel RATOG units under the rear fuselage when operating from small carriers.

Well-proportioned and purposeful in appearance, the **Yokosuka D4Y** possessed an excellent performance and owed much of its concept to the German He 118, the manufacturing rights for which Japan negotiated in 1938. Designed as a fast carrier-based attack bomber and powered by an imported Daimler-Benz DB 600G engine, the **D4Y1** was first flown in December 1941 and many were completed as dive-bombers. **D4Y1-C** reconnaissance aircraft were ordered into production at Aichi's Nagoya plant, the first of 660 aircraft being completed in the late spring of 1942. The first service aircraft were lost when the *Soryu* was sunk at Midway. Some 174 Suiseis of the 1st, 2nd and 3rd Koku Sentais were embarked in nine carriers before the Battle of the Philippine Sea; however, they were intercepted by American fighters long before reaching the American carriers, and suffered heavy casualties without achieving any success. A new version with 1,400-hp (1044-kW) Aichi Atsuta 32 engine appeared in 1944 as the **D4Y2** but, in the interests of preserving high performance, nothing was done to introduce armour protection for crew or fuel tanks, although a 13.2-mm (0.52-in) flexible gun (replacing the previous 7.92-mm/0.31-in gun) was included in the rear cockpit. Problems of reliability with the Atsuta inline engine led to adoption of a Kinsei 62 radial in the **D4Y3**, this engine being retained in 1945's **D4Y4**, a single-seat suicide dive-bomber. A total of 2,033 production D4Ys was completed.

Yokosuka D4Y 'Judy'

Specification:
Yokosuka D4Y3 'Judy'
Type: two-seat carrierborne dive-bomber
Powerplant: one 1,560-hp (1164-kW) Mitsubishi MK8P Kinsei 62 radial piston
Performance: max speed 357 mph (575 km/h) at 19,850 ft (6050 m); climb to 9,845 ft (3000 m) in 4.55 minutes; service ceiling 34,450 ft (10500 m); range 945 miles (1520 km)
Weights: empty 5,514 Lb (2501 kg); max take-off 10,267 Lb (4657 kg)
Dimensions: span 37 ft 8¾ in (11.50 m); length 33 ft 6¾ in (10.22 m); height 12 ft 3¼ in (3.74 m); wing area 254.03 sq ft (23.60 m²)
Armament: two fixed 7.7-mm (0.303-in) Type 97 machine-guns in nose and one 13.2-mm (0.52-in) Type 2 flexible gun in rear cockpit; 1,234 Lb (560 kg) of bombs

The D4Y2 variant of the Suisei (Comet) was fitted with the Aichi Atsuta 32 inline engine, an engine whose constant unserviceability plagued the early operational life of the aircraft until it was replaced by the Kinsei radial of the D4Y3. The type was codenamed 'Judy' by the Allies.

Index

Index

Picture credits:

The publishers wish to thank the following people and organisations for their help in supplying photographs for this book:
Bundesarchiv, Charles E. Brown Collection/Royal Air Force Museum, Fleet Air Arm Museum, Grumman, Imperial War Museum,
Lockheed, MacClancy Collection, McDonnell Douglas, United States Air Force, United States Navy.